Yaadgah

Yaadgah

Memories of Srinagar

Edited by
Arshi Javaid

YODA PRESS
C-28 Mayfair Gardens
New Delhi - 110016
www.yodapress.co.in

ISBN: 978-93-4856644-7

Editors in charge: Arpita Das, Tara Mathur and Ishita Gupta
Published by Arpita Das and Ishita Gupta for YODA PRESS

*To the memory of Srinagar's winding lanes
and whispering alleys,*

To the cherished Narwari Manzil of Lal Chowk.

*To Boba's animated laughter and the life
that revolved so warmly around her.*

Contents

Acknowledgements

This anthology is the culmination of a collective effort, standing on the unwavering support, guidance, and inspiration of numerous individuals and institutions.

First and foremost, my deepest gratitude goes to Prof. Dr. Nadja Christina Schneider, whose steadfast encouragement has shaped this project from its inception. Over the past four years, Nadja has hosted me in an intellectually stimulating environment at the Gender and Media Studies for the South Asian Region, Humboldt Universität zu Berlin. Her mentorship has been instrumental in enriching my academic journey. My association with the "Beyond Social Cohesion: Global Repertoires of Living Together" (RePLITO) project and the Dwelling Together: Urban Housing, Neighbourliness, and Multilocal Homemaking working group provided me with the framework and vocabulary to articulate concepts such as co-living and neighbourliness that had long simmered in my thoughts.

I am profoundly grateful to the Einstein Foundation Berlin and Humboldt Universität zu Berlin for their trust in this work and their support in bringing it to fruition.

To my teammates at GAMS and Dwelling Together: Urban Housing, Neighbourliness, and Multilocal Homemaking, thank you for exemplifying the power of weaving together marginalised narratives of communal living and social cohesion. Your influence has been transformative.

A special mention of appreciation is reserved for Anna Schneider, whose friendship has provided comfort during difficult times. This work wouldn't have seen the light of day if Riyaz-ul-Haque had not encouraged me to share this work with the world.

I am deeply indebted to my colleagues and friends at the Academy in Exile and Freie Universität Berlin for offering a sanctuary for free thought and exploration. Your camaraderie and insights have profoundly shaped the evolution of this anthology.

To the contributors and artists whose voices resonate through these pages, you are the soul of this work. Your art, stories, and reflections breathe life into these narratives. This anthology seeks to honour your resilience and the lived experiences of the communities it represents.

In Kashmir, I am profoundly appreciative of Zahid Ghulam Mohammed, Rashid Maqbool, Showkat A. Kathjoo, Showkat Nanda, Mir Khalid, Her Pixel Story, and the team at Shah-e-Hamdan School, Shopian for their time and collaboration.

I would also like to thank my editorial team at Yoda Press, Ishita Gupta and Tara Mathur, for their interest and enthusiasm for this project.

Finally, I express my heartfelt gratitude to my family. To my father, Javid Azar, who instilled in me a love for storytelling, and my mother, Abida, for her boundless affection. My grandmother, Shams-un-Nisa, enriched my life with her constant prayers. I am deeply thankful to my brother, Dawar, sister-in-law, Rabia, and niece, Yashal, for filling my life with joy. Above all, to my husband, Danish, I am most grateful for your steadfast support, which has been instrumental in my academic journey. This manuscript reached its final form alongside a beautiful new chapter in my life—the arrival of my daughter Arwa, during its editing phase. I hope she grows to embrace the magic of stories and storytelling.

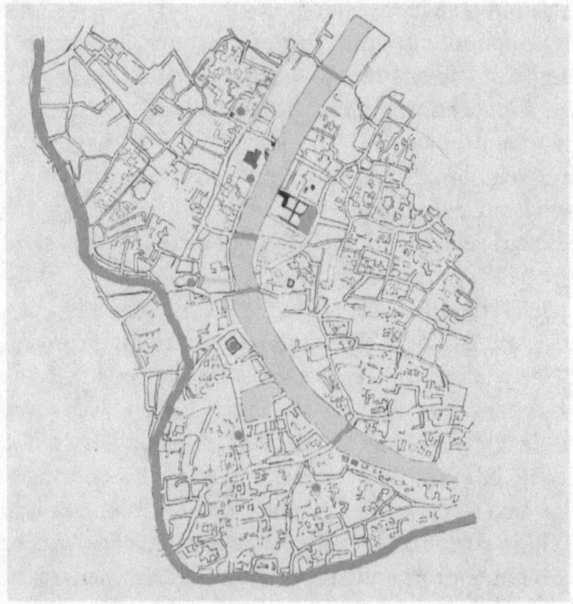

Tracing the contours of the Old City of Srinagar, one story at a time.
Map by Shajar Lateef, Salman Khursheed, & Adil Malik

Foreword

When Dr. Arshi Javaid contacted me in June 2021 in search of academic exchange with other scholars working on South Asia in German academia, she had already been in Berlin for a few months. At the time, she was a fellow in the Critical Scholarship Program at Freie Universität Berlin, where she was teaching and researching. Her work on the old city of Srinagar was met with great interest both from colleagues at our interdisciplinary Gender and Media Studies department for the South Asian Region (GAMS) at Humboldt-Universität zu Berlin, as well as in our transregionally oriented joint research project *Beyond Social Cohesion - Global Repertoires of Living Together* (RePLITO). We were all particularly intrigued to learn that Dr Javaid studied the everyday coexistence between Kashmiri Muslims and Kashmiri Pandits before the 1989 exodus of the latter. Among other interesting questions, she looked at food and eating habits as a central aspect of daily life as they had existed for a long time in the geographically close neighbourhoods of the old city of Srinagar. Another focus of her study was laid on the question of "How friendships and cordiality worked in this context of maintenance of strict boundaries and underlying tensions", as she put it. Arshi Javaid's approach, research interest, sense of responsibility and personal commitment to this project resonated well with RePLITO's focus on marginalised and neglected repertoires of living together as a starting point to rethink or decentre the concept of social cohesion from a transregional perspective.

The project, which ran from 2021 to 2024, engaged in comparative and cross-disciplinary research in Asia, Europe, Latin America, Africa as well as the Middle East. Our aim was to explore in-depth how social actors in different regions of the so-called Global South and within Europe's margins imagine and practice communal life and create bonds. These concepts and repertoires of living together were never taken for granted and continue to be negotiated and transformed in the context of dynamic interactions which often extend beyond localities, nation states or geographical regions, especially in times of increased mobilities and the digitalisation of almost all spheres of life. At the same time, it is interesting to note that *local* as well as *everyday* levels of interaction and participation, either in (post)conflict or in culturally, linguistically and religiously diverse contexts, have recently moved to the centre of discussions around the question whether forms of living together on equal terms and in mutual recognition of difference and plurality can or should even be 'cultivated'.

In view of these overlapping research interests and the many ethical questions that go hand in hand with them, Arshi Javaid's involvement in the RePLITO project was an obvious choice. In her role as a Visiting Research Fellow of the RePLITO project and member of the interdisciplinary working group *Urban Dwellings*, she contributed continuously to our stimulating academic exchange and many of our joint conference panels as well as other formats and activities. When Dr. Javaid's application as Einstein Junior Scholar to the Einstein Foundation Berlin was approved in spring 2023, she moved to the GAMS department with her *Yaadgah* project and has been working at the Institute for Asian and African Studies at HU Berlin ever since.

Concepts and repertoires of good coexistence, especially in regions and local contexts shaped by conflicts, inequalities and opposing identity and memory politics, these are existential questions for Dr. Javaid that motivate her academically and personally and move her deeply. She sees it as her responsibility, and a task that goes far beyond the scope of a funded research project to explore the many layers and nuances of these concepts and repertoires in more detail, and to preserve and convey this knowledge about living together in differences in the old city of Srinagar, to interested audiences both inside and outside Kashmir. In this endeavour, she finds herself in a race against the rapidly advancing and seemingly unstoppable transformation of Srinagar; what the old city of Srinagar will become and represent in the future, however, is currently forcibly decoupled from what it has been for many generations of residents. The memories of many individuals and families of these specific forms and practices of living together are firmly rooted in the local context—its neighbourhoods, the architecture and interiors of homes, the spiritual as well as the public meeting places—and at the same time shaped by and in relation to them. All our experiences are local, argues writer Taiye Selasi (2014), and she therefore suggests that we should not ask people about something as abstract as their national belonging (which is usually suggested by the question "where are you from?"), but rather where they see themselves as locals and what experiences are linked to the three Rs she describes as decisive for all our locally grounded experiences and memories: our relationships, rituals, and the restrictions we face in specific contexts.

Although Selasi's three Rs are not explicitly referred to in this anthology, they run like a connecting thread through the contributions collected here. Simultaneously, they seem to have formed the basis for this co-production of knowledge based on individual and joint experiences as well as memories passed on within the family to subsequent generations. When Arshi Javaid began her research for her *Yaadgah* project, she initially had a digital archive of memories in mind that would offer a wide range of opportunities for participation. In my view, however, it is a particular stroke of luck that her collaborative research practice in Srinagar also gave rise to the desire to create and publish this anthology. After having read her two wonderfully written contributions "*Habba Kadal*: What Was Left Behind in the mohallae" and "I have exiled my heart, for I have loved across boundaries", which we were able to publish first in the digital magazine of our department (*GAMSzine*), I became immediately aware that Arshi had already found her unique creative form of academic expression: a literarily inspired and empathic writing that enables new approaches to research-based knowledge and at the same time creates a shared space for emotions and solidarity. The anthology provides deep insights into the memories and knowledge of families, individuals, former neighbours or work colleagues and specific local forms of living and working together, from which a shared collective memory can emerge. This includes not only Kashmiri Muslims, but also Kashmiri Pandits who did not migrate in the wake of the 1989 exodus but stayed. As readers, we understand how significantly their lived everyday experiences differ from the mediated memories of the many Kashmiri Pandits who left Srinagar and who are often portrayed by the Indian media as the only representatives of this community.

Finally, two further aspects of this anthology should be mentioned: the precise description of the architecture (both from the outside and inside) and the intersectional gender perspective, through which we understand some of the differences regarding mobility and public urban space, as well as the everyday lives within residential buildings. The architectural lens, on the other hand, enables us to question and decentre a hegemonic view of the old city of Srinagar that has been shaped by tourism and the media. To do so, a different view of the architecture is required, informed by in-depth knowledge and lived experience, as assembled in this volume. In some of the contributions, the architecture or the material itself almost appears as an actor involved in this co-production of knowledge and collective memory-making, speaking both for itself and to the readers.

Prof. Dr Nadja-Christina Schneider
Professor of Gender and Media Studies
for the South Asian Region at
Humboldt-Universität zu Berlin.

Introduction

I arrived in Berlin in April 2021 with the nascent idea that I wanted to work around the multicultural neighbourhoods of the old city of Srinagar. I have grown up in one and carried it with me all through the years. It has been part of my everyday life. The neighbourhood was developed during the Afghan rule in Kashmir when the rulers decided to expand the city and establish alternate centres to circumvent the importance of the old city of Srinagar. Gradually, it expanded during the Sikh and Dogra rule. While some of the peripheries of our neighbourhood were developed for upmarket ruling patrons and the moneyed Khatri merchants, ours became a refuge primarily for working classes — many of them migrants coming through various waves of migration.

As the neighbourhood evolved under three distinct governing regimes, each characterised by differing religious affiliations, the *mohalla* (quarters) also exhibited a corresponding diversity on this front. However, what brought people together was a powerful sense of work ethic and co-living, making the mohalla home for everyone irrespective of where they came from. Such was the charm of Court Road, the mohalla where I grew up. When I share anecdotes of my neighbourhood with my friends—mainly other Kashmiris from different neighbourhoods or geographical locations—our experiences are very different. In many ways, this difference shapes our worldview politically and socially.

I often felt the urge to tell this story, but more urgent narratives from Kashmir took up space in my head, as well as in academic and literary spaces. The political chaos in the region never allowed one to sit back and think beyond the active violence. The distance that Berlin provided finally made me realise that conflict had also changed the spaces surreptitiously. It was essential to connect the dots between spaces, memory, and conflict, as well as placing the various agents vis-à-vis the spaces they retained and the social interactions they held.

Situated on the banks of river Jehlum[1], Srinagar is the product of historical interactions that have taken place over the years, from the significance of the Kashmiri Sultanate days (1339–1561), when the old city was formed, to the present day. Srinagar has always been the summer capital of Kashmir, and like all cities, it is not only a spatially bound geographical cluster, but also a cluster of social and political networks. Yet, it is crucial to distinguish the natural allure and geographical beauty of the city from the realities of daily life experienced by its inhabitants. Here, one confronts evident disparities manifested in varying sizes of houses, architectural styles, and the organisation of mohallas based on occupational similarities.

Corresponding to what is mentioned above, there is an accelerated transformation of Srinagar, where a remarkable change has occurred in terms of architecture, infrastructure, ownership, and demographic composition. This restructuring changes the political and social character of the city and is influenced by the interests of the state, the private sector, and the politically motivated interests of actors. Given the pace of change, it is essential to document the tangible and intangible aspects of endangered heritage, as well as the stories and narratives of those who lived or are currently living in the city, before everything evaporates in transition.

That is where the role of this small anthology comes in, undertaking an exercise where the past and contemporary become the key modalities to engage with the old city of Srinagar. The change urges one to take the old city seriously, and the socio-political crossroads where we stand, along with the frugality of both

1 This anthology intentionally employs the spelling Jehlum rather than the widely accepted Jhelum to reflect its colloquial pronunciation. The river originates in Kashmir, where it is referred to as Vyeth. In Sanskrit texts, it is known as Vitasta. Despite this, official documentation consistently uses Jhelum, likely a legacy of the non-Kashmiri dominance in the region's historiography and the colonial administration's preference for spellings aligned with their linguistic conventions. For instance, Varmul was altered to Baramulla, and Batamalun became Batamaloo during the colonial period.

academic and non-academic accounts vis-à-vis the city implore that some timely attention is paid. In Srinagar, the rise of 'urban' and 'newness' is fused with a sensorium of political language. We are noticing a rapid tempo of sensations that are being reproduced mechanically and digitally. Each day we see practices of new digital media that expose the city and its dwellers like commodities and territories of desire. Often reproducing misrepresentations, these practices violate people by creating harmful knowledge and turns the represented into a mute spectator (Sontag, 1977). Another essential argument that holds immense importance: who owns the city or who does the city belong to particularly in the times we live in? The question of what kind of city we live in cannot be divorced from what kind of social ties, relationships to nature, lifestyle technologies and aesthetic values we desire (Harvey, 2012). The right to city is far more than an individual liberty to access urban resources; the freedom to imagine and reimagine our cities is far more central. However, imagining cities is an act of invoking the past, present, and future, which is where the multiple essays in the anthology intervene. The writers have aimed to engage with the past, present and future through memories. While they constitute memories, cities serve as mnemonic aids as well. They remind us of our memories, both individual and collective but they also spur people to investigate broader societal maps they don't yet fully know. Whether one refers to "collective memory," "social memory," "public memory," "historical memory," "popular memory," or "cultural memory," most would agree with Edward Said that many 'people now look to this refashioned memory, especially in its collective forms, to give themselves a coherent identity, a national narrative, a place in the world' (Said, 1994). Memories and identities are often contested, hence the place of varied standpoints in the anthology.

Methodology

My engagement with the theme started with writing two short essays for my departmental magazine (*GAMSZINE*). Various conversations at my home institute, Gender and Media Studies for

South Asia Region, Institute for Asian and African Studies, Humboldt University, and Replito, a knowledge archive for Social Cohesion: Global Repertoires of Living Together (RePLITO), shaped this idea. However, things formally shaped after the Einstein Foundation showed interest in this work. Like many other projects, this one was conceived in a different format than what it would be. I arrived in Srinagar in August 2023 with a series of ideas for a website around the heritage of the old city of Srinagar, 3D mapping of the city, creating an audio-scape, and doing a couple of short films. However, very soon, I knew the city should decide how the project engages rather than vice versa. There was genuine fear after the abrogation of Article 370 in 2019, and inevitable fatigue had set in. So, I had to be patient and allow the city to speak to me however it wanted to. I started meeting friends and acquaintances and brought up the idea generally. Everyone I met had a personal story of the city, a memory they kept close to their hearts. Here, the city was coming to life through the characters I was looking for. So, I decided to collect the stories and decide later what to do with them. Women were particularly keen on taking on the idea quickly and writing down the city story from their vantage point, not only what they had seen but also what they had felt and experienced.

The next engagement was created with young artists who stepped in to draw the city as they perceived it because things were changing too fast. Together, we looked at the intimate street views, the brutal endurance of the crumbling city, its sights, sounds, and smells. One could not stop marvelling at the city's living force, its persistence and transitory nature, its histories and living stories at every alley. The walks were overwhelming and took over our senses, and soon enough, the boys sat down with their canvasses and colours to paint the city.

The artists at work, bringing visions of the city to life

Another significant engagement that contributed to creating this work were the long walks with women of different age groups through the city to understand its plurality and diversity and to reclaim it. The first walk was collaborated with *Her Pixel Story*, a feminist collective based in Srinagar. To our surprise, many young women joined in, chatted, laughed, shared kulfis and WhatsApp numbers, clicked pictures, and created joy on Srinagar streets on a sunny September day. Their social locations and clothing choices differed, but they all came together to imagine a radically different city. It was new to Srinagar because women don't flaneur;[2] their time schedules are marked between home and work or

---

2 The flâneur, traditionally depicted as the perceptive male observer of urban life, has dominated literary and cultural narratives for centuries. However, it's high time we acknowledge and celebrate the equally vital and transgressive role of the flâneuse. From Virginia Woolf to Martha Gellhorn, women have long been engaging in the nuanced exploration and documentation of city life, often overlooked in favour of their male counterparts. It's essential to recognize the invaluable contributions of these female flâneuses, whose keen insights and perspectives offer rich and multifaceted portrayals of urban landscapes, challenging traditional gender norms and expanding our understanding of urban experiences.

college. Forty minutes in public transport, then 30 more in Goni Khan market, where the dupatta has been given for colouring. It is essential to note here that the lives of women in Kashmir are not hijacked by ordinary patriarchy. The dangers created by the militarised conflict add to the misery.

We were stopped by curious onlookers who wondered what was happening. In an instance or two, security personnel intervened to ask if we were going to protest and that we should delete any pictures that had any security presence. We laughed together and drank tea at a café populated chiefly by men. The shop owner kindly asked his male clientele to make room for us. The roar of that laughter inspires this work in more ways than can ever be described.

However, this project also loomed through hiccups and ethical dilemmas. From the very start, I knew the project would be a collaborative effort, and it is essential to describe the nature of the collaboration. Though I have written the proposal and facilitated finances for the project, the project is based on collective creative efforts. I consider the contributors to be research companions who are as passionate about Srinagar as I am.

Earning trust in Kashmir is always tricky, and gaining confidence with Kashmiri Pandit families who had not migrated was an arduous exercise. However, I managed it through the help of local facilitators. The difficulty arose from an unimagined quarter, from one of my close Kashmiri Pandit friend's family who live in Delhi now. My friend wanted to associate with the project in a bigger role and wanted to travel to Srinagar. However, her family developed mistrust which spiralled into hate against me. During several phone calls, the family accused me of using the memory of co-living in a city to brainwash my friend, for turning her against the community and religion, for leading her on to the world of research and turning her away from the prospect of having an actual career. The list ran long, and so did the abuse. Accusations turned into screams and screams into open threats. I disconnected the call in horror, thinking how difficult it was working with a community that is considered a nemesis of mine. What had happened was a blow to what I had stood for all my life, the power of personal connections in resolving communal tensions, and here I was, wondering what had gone wrong.

Despite the shortcomings, the work is a labour of love for our beloved city Srinagar and is distributed in written and visual sections. The sections are thematically organised and are called Those Who Never Left, Seeking Home, Yaarbal (Meeting Point) and Shelters of Solace.

Artwork by Adil Malik

1

Those Who Never Left

1

Habba Kadal: What Was Left Behind in the mohallae

Arshi Javaid

There is an exceptional quality to this part of the city. I arrive here on a September evening, when the days have grown considerably shorter. The flickering lamps glow in the kitchens, where dinner has been cooked long ago, sometimes in the late afternoon or even earlier. Traditionally, in Kashmiri households, food is cooked early, mostly based on the power cut schedule. Like in other parts of South Asia, electricity is rationed in Kashmir despite the region being a major producer of hydroelectricity.

I walk through the narrow lanes of Habba Kadal asking shopkeepers where Suman Pandita's house is. For there can be no confusion here; there are not many Suman Panditas around since not many *Battea*/Kashmiri Pandit families stayed behind through the chaos of 1990. "Go on walking straight, then take a right, you will see a newly constructed house on your right side. They have a cherry-coloured gate and a small provision store opposite the house. But why do you want to go there?" asks one of them. "Ah, I am a researcher and have been in touch with the family lately. I am trying to understand mohallae (neighbourhood) and what happened to mixed community mohallae once the Kashmiri Pandits left," I blurt out immediately, fearing the obvious sensitivities that come around when working with a microscopic minority of Kashmiri Pandits who did not migrate out of the Kashmir valley. The Kashmiri Pandit Sangharsh Committee (KPSS), an organisation that represents the Kashmiri Pandits who did not migrate to Jammu or southwards towards mainland India, puts the number of the remaining community members close to 3000.[3]

---

3 In 2011, Sanjay Tickoo, president of Kashmiri Pandit Sangharsh Committee gave the number close to 3400 in an *Al Jazeera* story. In an interview with me in September 2021, he places the numbers around 3000. He says that the

A young boy who must have been born in the early 2000s joins the conversation with a certain sense of honour and tells me, "It's *naar* everywhere (meaning 'the earth is spitting fire'). Don't you know the Battea chemist Bidroo was killed by unknown gunmen a few weeks ago in broad daylight at his shop, so we get alarmed when anyone asks around for this family. You should also research something else. The policemen in civil dress keep a watch on everyone who visits them, but unidentified gunmen still have their way."

I walk through the guided path thinking about the measurement of the space and events of the past. I look at the height of the termite-eaten wooden lamp posts and feel that the mohalla is languishing and degenerating. The glum desperation of marginalisation and police repression reflected through the bullet holes in many of the walls of the mohalla and the inability of the inhabitants to get the structures refurbished. In some cases where renovation was done, the cheap building material tells the untold story. I try to take my mind off all this and think of the tilt of the bodies of stray cats, preying on a bunch of sparrows swinging on low-lying electric wires.

I reach the door of the Panditas' house and find it locked. A huge classic Aligarh lock gives a sense of completion to the act of locking. I hear a woman calling out to me from the *kaeni* (attic) of another house, asking me to knock at the back door. "They have not kept the front door open, ever since *halaat* (conditions) intensified in the last weeks." I knew what she was referring to and made haste to the back door of the cemented house the Panditas had constructed.

I knock at the door and give my references to Suman's mother Phamb. She and the house cats take me to the guest room. I try to be cat-friendly to permeate the thickness of the situation. Phamb asks for my preference of tea, assuming Lipton (brewed sugar tea) would be the answer. I ask for *kehva* instead, which was not even offered. The kehva served in Battae households is quite different

---

intensity of events of new age militancy in 2016 and the abrogation of Article 370 in 2019 led to further migrations. For more, see https://www.aljazeera.com/news/2011/8/2/kashmiri-pandits-why-we-never-fled-kashmir(last accessed: May 9, 2022)

from how it is made in the households of Kashmiri Muslims.[4] She gathers the kehva ingredients and puts them to brew in the kitchen, asking her grand-daughter to serve it once it is brewed. Phamb was my mother's work colleague some years ago. "Your mother is a nice and simple woman; hardworking too. She has remained honest throughout the job," while the granddaughter Veda joins in with kehva.[4] We take our respective cups and, in a moment of absolute stillness I deviate to the depth of the cup, the myriad ripples at the bottom. I wake up from the repetitive depth and ripple cycle and ask abruptly "How was living here when everyone left?"

Phamb did not have to think a lot before she responded, "It was eerie and silent. I could not leave for personal reasons. I was a young widow with three children, had no resources to migrate out and start a new life somewhere else. *Yeti aes panin jai* (we owned the house), had a roof to protect my children and the familiarity of the old neighbourhood. What could a young widow do in a *wopar* (foreign) place? I knew how the school system worked here. I could send them to a school, if not a private one like M Das, but the public one at Babapora. And then I had the solace of the fact that if ever my son fell into bad company or smoked clandestinely in the by-lanes outside, the neighbours would inform me or correct his behaviour. What would I have done in Jammu, if Suman fell in the *suhbat* (company) of *badmaash* (licentious) Dogras (a Rajput Hindu group in Jammu)," she says in a mild manner that was self-assuring too.

All her relatives from her maiden family as well as her in-laws had migrated out. Phamb *never* regretted her decision of not

---

4   In Kashmir, Kehva is a traditional tea prepared with tea leaves, either green or black, and a wide variety of condiments. The condiments are decided according to the occasion. A classic kehva served at home is a brew of black tea/ Bombay chai, cardamom, cinnamon and sugar. It is brewed till it achieves a red hue. If the kehva is made for guests, saffron strands are brewed with green cardamoms, de-skinned almonds and sugar. For festive gatherings and weddings, saffron, green cardamoms, deskinned grained almonds and milk is brewed together till it achieves a thick consistency. Traditionally, the kehva was made with eleven ingredients, keh signifying eleven in Kashmiri. The significant difference between the kehva served in the Battea and the Muslim households is the difference of tea leaves. Muslims use black tea, while Battea use green tea. It is exclusively boiled with green cardamoms and green tea, giving a greenish hue to Battea kehva.

moving out. Despite the regular jibes her migrated relatives throw at her for choosing to live in "Pakistan", for risking her safety, she draws comfort from the fact that her children received an education and also got into government service jobs. Now, her three grandchildren go to the poshest English missionary schools in the city. There has been a certain upward mobility for the family and they have also been able to construct a house in reinforced cement concrete. Phamb hurries up and calls her grandson to take me to another Battea household in the mohalla. She tells me "Everyone who stayed behind has a different story. For that matter, the Muslims who did not move out to the outer developing areas, also have a story."

2

I have exiled my heart;
I loved across boundaries

Arshi Javaid

Part 1

In the twilight hours of a rainy March evening in 2022, a security alert chimed on the computers of the police and surveillance grid in Kashmir. It was an SOS call that needed to be addressed quickly. Allegedly, a 17-year-old boy from the Kashmiri Pandit community had been kidnapped by militants. He had left home for school, but did not return at the scheduled hour.

After the abrogation of Article 370 in 2019, there was a new wave of targeted killings of Kashmiri Pandits by unknown gunmen. In Kashmir, unknown gunmen are a shadowy phenomenon. With such a thick ratio of armed personnel vis-à-vis civilians, unknown gunmen appear and kill people like wanton boys kill flies. And in the world's largest security zone, none of the unknown gunmen could ever be traced.

The boy in the picture had left home for tuition in the morning, but did not return at the scheduled hour. The family called the school to know the boy's whereabouts, only to find that he had never reached school that day; his friends were called but nobody knew where the boy was. Where could a 17-year-old have gone, if not kidnapped or taken hostage by militants? Soon the news spread widely and was carried by news portals. Within no time, a hashtag campaign was started by the Pandit community outside Kashmir. The community members in Kashmir expressed fear and resentment at not being provided ample security by the state.

Part 2

The next morning the IG police addressed a press conference congratulating his team and the IT cell for rescuing the boy within no time. He also revealed that the case was not militancy related. However, very soon, the favourable hashtags began peddling hate against the boy in the picture. "Punish the boy" and "Shame on you" were some keywords.

Part 3

Sometime in November of the same year, Ragini walked me to the house of Ayush, the boy who was allegedly kidnapped. We entered a newly constructed house where the boy's mother was mopping the floor. With her frail structure, she was rearranging the shoes on the front balcony, putting them in a queue like disciplined students. One look at us and she tells Ragini that everything in the house needs to be sorted and systemised regularly, each and everything requires her careful attention. We offered to visit later, but she directed us to a room where she would join us after she finished the chores. Meanwhile, her sister-in-law, drenched, arrives to tell her she is cleaning the washrooms of the house. She says to us before heading out to clean again: "Our children make this space a garbage house. We find it hard to tidy and reorganise everything."

Razdan worked very hard to construct this house after they brought down the worn-out structure they inherited from their father. The new house consisted of several rooms overcome by objects, wearing its own viscera on the outside: utensils, tape recorders, a DVD player, an LED television, computer monitor, and other gadgets were scattered around the house. The family did not think of migrating out in the 1990s because their ailing old mother wanted to live her last years in Kashmir. The Razdan brothers also envisioned a certain financial prosperity in staying back.

They had jobs and were skilful too, so they could get private assignments after work hours. A migrated life would not have been as useful, Razdan would often tell their children.

We enter a room and find Ayush sitting there. He seems to be distant from the cleaning choir. With his symmetrical chiselled features, wide forehead, and well-groomed clean skin, Ayush bears a striking resemblance to Asim Azhar, a Pakistani singer and actor. As he introduces himself and his educational journey, a certain innocence radiates from his eyes. He whispers about the need to be focused on his goals and how important it is to make up for lost time as he has just returned from the Juvenile Home. Another stark realisation he shares is to listen to parents and prioritise them over everyone else. He asks Ragini if he can confide in me and share his story. Apparently, Ragini, my interlocuter, had taken a hard-line position against the community when tough times fell on Ayush.

In 2016, Ayush met a girl on Instagram. Weeks and weeks of talking converged into a secret love affair. Passions ran high with each passing day, but it was difficult for the two to meet in person as Srinagar rarely opened in the first months of their courtship. They had begun talking after the commander Burhan Wani was martyred, and for months, a curfew was imposed in Kashmir. When things began to normalise, they decided to meet, but their backgrounds were too contentious to meet in public. After all, everyone in the mohalla knew Ayush was from one of the few remaining Kashmiri Pandit families and Rosheeba had a Muslim background. If spotted together they could arouse unnecessary attention. So, the two decided to delay the meeting as long as possible, but Ayush ensured he walked around Rosheeba's house each day to catch a glimpse of her or wait at the bus stop which Rosheeba passed through. The love blossomed through shared horoscopes, food recipes, favourite songs and inspiring quotations on Instagram. As it became difficult to stay apart, the two decided they should perhaps meet in the Civil Lines area where nobody knew them. The two started meeting frequently in cafes in the Civil Lines area, defying the familiar gaze while becoming part of the invisible matrix of the outer part of the city.

As the relationship went along, both were clear that they would elope as soon as they were legally adults. There was no future for them other than eloping, as the families and communities would not have accepted the relationship under any circumstances. But the plot did not move as expected. Someone from Rosheeba's extended family spotted her with Ayush in Civil Lines. They had suddenly become visible through invisibility. To make things worse, the identifier knew Ayush by face and family name for he had seen him strolling in the mohalla. The news reached both families and there was an uproar. Rosheeba was locked in, her phone was snatched by the family, and she was not allowed to meet anyone.

Days and days passed without any news of her. Ayush was consumed and devastated when a new idea struck him: to fake a break-up so Rosheeba's movement out of the house would be restored, and to elope as soon as things moved to normalcy. They could not wait to become adults legally; the circumstances had changed for them suddenly. Soon a break-up was faked and a cooling period of a few months was put in place so that Rosheeba's family would stop monitoring her. As soon as their grip loosened, the two decided to pretend to leave for school and fly to New Delhi. Ayush had kept logistics ready: he had saved some money over the years, stolen a piece of his mother's jewellery which he pawned to buy the flight tickets and to pay for other expenses.

The plan was to reach Delhi and get married as soon as possible. The second step was to find a job in a call centre which hired people based on matriculation. It started snowing the morning they were supposed to take the flight. Ayush joked to Rosheeba that when Shiva and Parvati got married, it snowed, so this was a good omen. However, it turned out to be not so good an omen; all the outbound and inbound flights from the Srinagar airport were cancelled that day. In Kashmir, life comes to a standstill with the slightest weather changes. The two decided to take the first flight the next morning and took refuge in a nearby hotel. With their mobile phones off, they had disconnected from the madness of the practical world, to slip into a surreal corner. Tears trickle from Ayush's eyes as he vents the memory of the moment. "Whenever we held hands before we were scared to be spotted by relatives and acquaintances. This was the first time we held hands without any fear. It felt like our skin was sinning and liberating itself of the baggage too."

They were anguished that the flight did not take off but were hopeful that by the next morning, they would be away from there to a place where their religious differences would evaporate. They waited for the night to pass. However, the happiness was short-lived. Soon there was a knock on the door and all hope of love was lost for them. Ayush's family had informed the police that their son had gone missing for a few hours, and they suspected he had been kidnapped by militants. A high alert was initiated and a community vigil was launched through a virtual medium. So that the office of the Home Minister for the Indian State got involved and directed that the case should be taken up on a priority basis. Ayush and Rosheeba were located the same night and by midnight, they were under police custody. Both were taken to a magistrate where Rosheeba cried out loudly that she loved Ayush and the day she becomes an adult, she would marry him under the Special Marriage Act. She also disclosed that she had eloped consensually and was not kidnapped by him.

While Rosheeba was taken by her family, troubles weren't over for Ayush. Ayush's family was worried that the Muslim community might come out against him. However, something else happened, the Pandit community wanted to punish Ayush for trespassing. He had brought shame and dishonour to the community. The family was cast out. His parents feared that if Ayush was taken home, he might be attacked by the remaining Pandit community. They appealed to the judge to lodge Ayush in a juvenile centre till the community rage abated. A meeting was organised in the nearby temple complex to teach a lesson to erring youngsters like Ayush. The family had to discontinue their visits to the temple for the scorn they met there.

Everything came crashing down and both of them became strangers to one another. The love was crystallised in religion, from an infidel's love to a transgressor's love. I look at Ayush, whose eyes have widened by now. "It's perfect emptiness, the ideal vacuum, but some day my community will have to answer as to why they boycotted me and my family. There have been rare instances where people were involved in cross-religious relationships, but maybe some of them are braver than us. Age and class are on their side."

He ends the conversation saying, "I have exiled my heart, for I loved across boundaries."

3

Ragini: The Story and the Storyteller

Arshi Javaid

Phamb asks her grandson Yug to take me to Ragini Didi's house. Her family is another that has not migrated. We cross the old Habba Kadal bridge and slowly walk towards the Karfalli mohallae. As a child, I was always told how this bridge bustled with people in mornings and afternoons, office goers, students and hawkers alike. The bridge refashioned itself each day, like a *juloos* had taken it over.

This bridge formed an important transition point between work and the repetitive rhythm of everyday where people woke up between crumpled sheets and washed themselves with newly unwrapped cakes of soap, eating the basic lunch of rice and curry at unusual hours.[5] Before leaving, many of them took an update from the daily *khabarnama* broadcast by Radio Kashmir or the more boisterous ones kept themselves occupied with the latest songs played by *Akashvani*. Not so long ago, the bridge had been a destination for merchants who gathered at every solstice and equinox with their cargo of ground ginger and mustard oil, beads and threads, poppy seeds and raisins. From here the goods were circulated to the internal markets of the neighbourhoods.

Yug and I walk over the squeezed tubes of toothpaste, blown-out bulbs, newspapers and candy wrappers. The city cleaners have gone on another strike for better wages. In Srinagar city, cleaners share a strange relationship with city dwellers. On regular days they are derisive *watals* (a caste group involved in cleaning), but after festive occasions, they are welcomed like angels

---

5 Many Kashmiris who were employed with the government offices would eat their lunch in the morning before leaving for work. Breakfast would be a cup of salted tea with a piece of bread at dawn after the *fajr* prayers while piping hot rice and curry was mostly eaten before 9 a.m.

who expel, discard, and cleanse the recurrent stacks of garbage and residues of yesterday's existence.

Yug tells me he doesn't remember the way clearly, and he should ask Ragini to send us the WhatsApp location. However, instead of sending the location, Ragini emerges to escort us home. When I glance at her she tells me she has not been keeping well, and that is why she has been in her pyjamas till afternoon. "Despite being ill, I could not have said no to meeting you as Yug brought you here. *Mye chu yi warai toath* (I am very fond of him)," she tells me as we walk towards her house. We walk through crammed narrow streets as unexplained gazes and stares assail us. If you are not from the mohallae or regular to the place, it is common for neighbours to get inquisitive. While some eyes stare at you as if they recognise you, some demand recognition in your eyes. One has barely arrived in the mohallae and is already one of them, gone over to their side, absorbed in the kaleidoscope of eyes, wrinkles and grimaces.

We walk into a decrepit house made of mud and *maharaji* bricks. The house has a big enough *aangan* (courtyard) which is uncommon in the old city. There is a pallid decadence around. She takes us into a living space which is separated from the kitchen through a *baam* (frontal architectural façade). It's an unusual old house emanating a sense of unrest from every corner. There are cracks in the beams and the cornices. Ragini's mother Priya is sitting in the same room watching a series on *Star Plus* while also heating her feet with an ivory-blue rubber water bag. I look around the room we are seated in. A discernible penury whispers from every corner, the tattered matting, the walls falling to pieces. I initiate pleasantries with Priya but she doesn't reciprocate; Ragini instead takes to the task of communicating for all of us. She tells Yug that she purchased a new phone for Rs 35,000 and has a new sim card too. In the same breath, she goes on to say she would have shown the new phone to us, but as there is no electricity in the room upstairs, she would show it another time. She reveals how Yug's family came together for them when her father, Mr. Kaul, died suddenly in Jammu. "He had gone for a wedding and never returned. Can you believe what kind of misfortune broke on us? It was a heart attack, a massive one. Some people had to go to Jammu to get his dead body." She taps the middle of her forehead with her forefingers to indicate the magnitude of loss," *Taqseer bai kya*. (Misfortune, what else), *Bhagwan* did not have any mercy on us, we are original Shaivaites, not like the new ones who took up the Koul surname in order to gentrify, or like those who fled Shiva's abode. Do you know there is a difference between Kouls and Kauls?

"My cough has not gone either," she blurts suddenly. "A few days before his death, my father had yellow eyes, a growth of beard of a man who looked like a revered pir," she adds.

As she oscillates between mourning her father, the veracity of being a Kaul, and coughing, getting some tea for us catches her attention. Instantly she is reminded there is no milk in the house and she would have to fetch some milk from the stores. I suggest we all could have kehva as the condiments are mostly available in Kashmiri houses. She starts brewing the kehva but keeps on apologising for not being able to serve special confectionaries meant to be served to guests. She serves the kehva with basic Battae Kashmiri bread[6] and urges us to have it giving her own *qasam* (oath) to me and Yug. All this while, her mother stays glued to the television screen.

I try to steer the conversations to mohallae and the common living, away from the world of gadgets. I introduce my life in the mohalla not so long ago, before my parents moved to the suburbs and how my family has not been able to leave the place emotionally. For the next few seconds, Ragini and I speak about the positive aspects of living in old neighbourhoods and how the experience is valuable in its own way. "But I want to enjoy life and flee these restrictions that come with this life. I also want to wear Western clothes and not look like a *behenji* (someone who is not fashionable). This Diwali, I plan to buy only Western

---

6 Between Kashmiri Muslims and Kashmiri Pandits, there weren't any particular inter-dining traditions. Sometimes men shared meals at weddings or functions, but women I have come across said they shared raw stuff but never cooked meals. Sometimes one's class location also decides the inter-dining patterns, partial or full.

　　Since bread dough is kneaded by hands, community bakers from one's own community would be trusted with it. Hence the presence of religion-based bakers. However, butchers were always Muslim, implying the principle of raw and cooked. Commonly one hears that soaked walnuts were exchanged on Shivratri, which again was an uncooked gift.

clothes, so that I can use them in Delhi. I am tired of living in Kashmir, we have seen a very harsh life here; nobody can imagine what we underwent. There were only empty houses and ghostly silences around, nobody to call our own. We went to a nearby Battae school and my mother would keep coming through the day to check on us. She dropped us off in the morning, then got us lunch and finally came to pick us up. There was *dehshat* (fear) around. Everyone had left, only a handful of us were here. The nature of my father's job did not allow us to leave, but those who left never asked about our well-being. All our relatives left, but never cared to ask how were we doing. Instead, they waited for postcards with our death news to arrive," she pronounces in an agitated manner.

By now I observe a pattern in Ragini's conversations. They grow in concentric circles like the trunk of a tree, each circle showing a certain ambivalence towards the other, nonetheless significant to the tree. I knew Ragini was my story and my story-teller. "Why would they wait for death," I ask her. "Why not, it justifies their decision to move out. You have no idea what jibes were thrown at us who stayed back. We were regularly told by our migrated Pandit community, that you could stay back because your women were involved in licentious relations with the Muslim militants. That is why they allowed you to stay. Sometimes they accuse us of financially supporting the militancy. What did we get in the end; the jobs and residential quarters are reserved for Pandits who migrated. Non-migrant *battas* don't exist for the state and the Prime Minister. What did we get by choosing to stay back in our motherland? *Darbadari* (waste of time)."

Though there have been some organisations run by non-migrant Kashmiri Pandits, their demands have not been mirrored by national media or fulfilled through the central state policy. "Nobody stood by us. They hired the migrant Pandits through the reserved job quota and provided them with securitised housing, either in temples or the housing enclaves established for them. Do I or my brother not deserve a job? We are well qualified. Are we not *naukri layak*? My brother works for a private company for a meagre salary of Rs 5000. But then you know we are lesser Pandits, not blue eyed like those who migrated," she asks angrily.

State help has been an illusory envelope for those who did not migrate. I ask her about the Muslim neighbours who lived around. She interrupts me to say, "The *asli* (true) neighbours have given me so much love, some of them call me *kacher* (blonde) and for some, I am an angel. They consider me lucky and auspicious. For example, if they are using a new gadget or they get a new bike, they will always ask me to touch it or bless it with my prayers. You know I am very religious and have a deep connection to *maata raani* (Hindu goddess), people feel my spirituality when I am connected to them. I am godmother to many children in the neighbourhood." While Ragini says all of this in an unusual matter-of-fact tone, for me it is indicative of something having gone awry.

I ask her the definition of asli neighbours and who they are. "Asli neighbours are those who originally belonged to the neighbour- hood and did not move in later, who were asli *baskeendars* (inhabi- tants) and not *haenz* (lake or water body dwellers) who came from Dal." Ragini imagines that the character of the neighbourhood was changed by the influx of new inhabitants because they did not understand the value and ethics of mohallae. "They are *fitnal* (vile) and *ladiegirs* (quarrelsome) and sometimes the women are loose, while the asli ones could be *safeed posh* (poor) but dignified. The new ones outnumber those who are asli. But there would be *insaaf* (justice) one day, the baser ones will be held accountable. There will be justice from Bhagwan."

As we sip the kehva, I request Ragini to help me in meeting the other Battaea families around the old city. She sketches a tentative itinerary of whom she would introduce me to, and which families we would visit together. As we talk about these details, we notice fumes of bitter smoke in the room. Ragini's mother has put a caul- dron of mustard oil on the boil. The smoke leaves us all coughing and teary-eyed. On a very abrupt note, we call off the meeting with the promise of meeting again the next day and resuming our conversation.

Post Script

I have known Ragini for over three years. This essay was written when we met for the first time. Over the years, what kept coming up in conversations was a huge sense of powerlessness induced by personal circumstances, and the political and social apathy of co-religionists. For the first two years, Ragini did not own a smartphone and was not on WhatsApp. Sometimes she would borrow a phone from the shopkeeper near her house to make a WhatsApp call to me abroad. However, she never told me why she made calls from the shopkeeper's number, and would instead say that her phone did not have enough credit or the battery crashed the previous night. This was constant. Our conversations were short and strange, where she displayed a deep desire for mobility, to wear modern clothes, to move out of mohalla. In 2024, Ragini finally managed to get a smartphone, from which she frequently texts that she is planning to go to Mumbai to join the Hindi film industry or that she will go to Gulmarg with her friends and party at the Gulmarg club that night or any other thing, which shows that her lifestyle has changed. On most days, Ragini displays a certain eccentricity, sometimes telling me the family is now a millionaire as they have sold the old house in mohalla and moved to Rajbagh (a posh Srinagar neighbourhood). Ragini's eccentricity is a silent form of resistance by building a new world in her head until nothing may harm her, neither poverty and helplessness nor fear.

Artwork by Adil Malik

2

Seeking Home

4

Absence

Mehar Qadri

Melancholy, an emotion woven from the delicate strands of yearning, reaches into the hidden depths of our souls like tendrils of mist on a moonlit night. It is a feeling that envelops us, suffocating, leaving us gasping for an air of solace. When something vanishes, it leaves behind a void, yawning like a gaping maw, echoing with the silent screams of longing. We find ourselves adrift, reaching out for the intangible—a lost love, a cherished memory, or perhaps just a fragment of ourselves. It is a longing that devours us from within, leaving us stranded like shipwrecked sailors, clawing at the shadows of what once was. Yet, this ache resides deep within, unseen and unfathomable, defying our attempts to articulate its depths.

The house in this story stands as a sentinel of solitude, its weary form weathered by the relentless assault of time. Its corners, like forgotten whispers, hold the weight of countless memories, heavy with the burden of longing. The cracks in its mud walls resemble the wrinkles etched upon the face of an ancient sage, each line a testament to the passage of years.

In a valley where the earth swallows memories whole, who pauses to acknowledge the weary sighs of a solitary dwelling? And yet, if one listens closely, the house speaks. Its dusty interiors, bathed in the soft glow of twilight, whisper secrets of separation that defy human understanding. It is a place haunted by absence, where the echoes of lost laughter linger like ghosts in the shadows, a silent witness to the ache of yearning for those who have slipped beyond the veil of time.

An abandoned house waits for no one, its weathered frame standing sentinel against the passage of time. Yet, after 13 years, two souls found themselves standing before its weary door, gazing upon it as if witnessing a rare apparition. The door, creaking shut like the final chapter of a forgotten tale, sealed the house off from the outside world, enclosing within its walls the silent vigil of years gone by.

As we wandered through the labyrinthine alleys of downtown Srinagar, the air pulsed with the haunting melody of the Maghreb azaan, reverberating like an ancient hymn weaving through the city's cobblestone streets. It was as though the very atmosphere was charged with sacred energy, urging us onward in our pilgrimage to Moghal Masse's house.

I recall how we moved in silent synchrony, our eyes fixed ahead, and each step echoing softly against the ancient stones beneath our feet. There was a palpable tension in the air, as if the streets themselves held their breath in anticipation of our arrival.

Faces passed us by, some veiled in the cloak of ignorance, others clouded with disbelief. For 13 long years, Moghal Masse had faded into the tapestry of forgotten souls, her memory obscured by the relentless march of time. Yet, amidst the sea of indifferent faces, there lingered a silent longing, a yearning for recognition that pulsed beneath the surface like a hidden current. And so, we pressed on, guided by an unseen hand towards our destination. Each alleyway we traversed felt like a journey into the unknown, a pilgrimage through the shadows of memory and longing. And as we stood before the abandoned house, its weathered walls bearing silent witness to the passage of time, we couldn't help but feel the weight of history pressing down upon us, urging us to remember, to bear witness to the forgotten stories that lay buried within its crumbling embrace.

Case History and Context

Nazir Ahmad Teli, a teacher by profession, in his early twenties, left for school in 1991 and was never seen again. Moghal Masse, a single mother to an only son, became one of the first members of a brave initiative of several thousand women called APDP (The Association of Parents of Disappeared Persons), whose young sons or husbands have been subjected to enforced disappearance by police or Armed Forces protected by the Armed Forces Special Powers Act (AFSPA). Since then, she has searched every police station and army camp to trace her only son. Moghal Masse's search for her only son ended when she breathed her last in the fall of 2009, after 19 years of searching.

This is a story of the erasure of Moghal Masse and many like her who withered away and disappeared in an unending wait for their loved ones. Their bodies transformed into an intimate landscape of memory and war.

During our search for the house where she once lived, we passed by an Imambara (a shrine built by Shia Muslims for congregational mourning) with black flags bearing the words "Ya Hussain A. S.".[7] I couldn't help but think about how Hussain symbolises sacrifice and how Karbala teaches us about remembrance. Suddenly, a soft voice from behind asked us what we were looking for. The woman who spoke to us was younger than most of the people we had asked for directions, yet she knew where Moghal Masse used to live.

"Yes, she was our neighbour," she said. "A kind lady who lived alone for a very long time. Come, I'll take you to her house."

As we walked through the tiny lanes of our final destination, the grey hues of an autumn evening had already taken over. We stopped at a shop to ask for directions again. A customer gladly offered to lead us to the house but informed us that it had been bought by a neighbour. As we entered the renovated tiny lane with a mosaic of yellow and red tiles, we took a right turn and saw the house we had been searching for.

I felt my legs getting heavier as I leaned against a nearby wall. The man accompanying us asked if the house had any significance to us, but we had no answer. Nobody had visited the house or come looking for Moghal Masse since her death 13 years ago. After a brief pause, Showkat saw the confusion on the man's face and explained that we were documenting cases like hers. Showkat took out his camera and started taking pictures of the locked wooden door. We left as night fell, and I returned home feeling transfixed, heavy-hearted, and even a little guilty.

---

7 Alia Salam (A.S.) is a respectful and reverential phrase in Islamic tradition, meaning "peace be upon him". It is commonly used after mentioning Prophets, Imams, Imamzadas and angels.

Photographs by Showkat Nanda

The next day, we visited the current owners of the house. As I greeted them with salaam, the women in the small court-yard seemed confused as to why we would want pictures of a ruined house that nobody had lived in for 13 years. A young girl named Amaara was given the task of showing us around. As the main door of Moghal Masse's house wouldn't open, she led us through an adjoining door between the houses. We entered a courtyard full of junk and a few chickens roaming around. As Amaara struggled to open the huge iron lock on an old wooden door, I took off my shoes. The door opened to reveal the ruins of a two-story traditional mud house, like a dark dungeon full of cobwebs.

In its heyday, this ruin was a home filled with life, hope, and laughter. The basement was used to store wood and grain for the harsh winter. Amaara warned that it was dusty and that I should wear my shoes, but we are taught never to enter a revered place or a shrine with our shoes on. This house was Moghal Masse's only companion for 19 years in her search for her son until her death. It embodied everything that she had lived through. I entered barefoot.

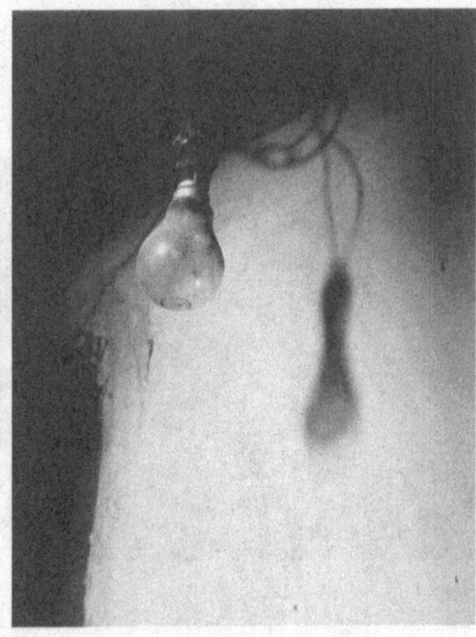

Photographs by Showkat Nanda

As you step inside, a cold and dry scent hits your senses, evoking the feeling of a desert on a long, chilly winter night. The place seems abandoned, with no sign of life in sight. The first emotion that washes over you is abandonment. To the left is a muddy stairwell leading to a door and a small square carved out in the wall supports the stairwell, letting in the only source of light in the house. The door opens into a kitchen where Moghal Masse spent her entire life.

Though the room is the same, it is now filled with rubber pipes, paint boxes, rags, and three shut wooden windows that let in streaks of light. Everything seems unfamiliar to her memories, almost like a sort of erasure. However, as soon as you touch the mud walls, she comes to life. Even though you can't see her or the life she lived in that room, she is everywhere, unseen yet omnipresent, almost godly. She serves as a reminder of the 8000 (and counting) enforced disappearances, and she, along with hundreds like her, is an undeniable part of our history and memory.

APDP

The Association of Parents of Disappeared Persons (APDP) is a collective of relatives of victims of enforced and involuntary disappearances in Kashmir. In many cases, these disappearances end in extra-judicial killings or death by torture. Formed in 1994, the APDP organises efforts to seek justice and information about the whereabouts of missing family members. It currently consists of family members of about a thousand victims and actively campaigns to end the practice and crime of involuntary and enforced disappearances on local, national, and international platforms. Since 1989, APDP members have been engaged in documenting enforced disappearances in Kashmir and have collected information on over a thousand such cases so far. On the 10th day of each month, families of the disappeared gather under the aegis of APDP to hold a public protest in Srinagar to commemorate the disappearance of their loved ones and to seek answers from the state about the whereabouts of the missing persons.

It had been some time since we stepped into the house, yet everything still felt fresh—the hues, the scents, the sounds. As we neared dusk the creaking of the balcony floorboards interrupted our work. I couldn't quite discern whether it was a cry, a wail, or a silent plea for us to depart. We retreated to the courtyard of the new owners, where we encountered a frail, elderly woman seated on the cement porch. She ask Amaara about us, and as I approached, she took my hand, inviting me to sit beside her.

Her name was Khaje, and she confided in me about her deep bond with Moghal Masse—they were childhood friends who had played together, married around the same time, and later, she bore witness to her friend's profound loneliness. Gesturing to a small window adorned with wooden bars, Khaje revealed that they spent countless hours conversing through it during the final years of Moghal Masse's life. When Amaara mentioned our visit to the graveyard, Khaje's eyes brimmed with memories of their enduring friendship and inevitable separation. Drawing me closer, she whispered, *"depzes khejan wonnai b yimai wean jaldi. Wean gov waariyah kaal."* (Tell her, Khaje said I will come soon. It has been long).

As she tenderly kissed my forehead, we embarked on our journey to find the graveyard. In Kashmir, graveyards hold profound political significance. Not a single one exists without a martyr resting within its grounds. These burial sites serve as tangible milestones of our collective memory. Each of us carries a distinct emotion or memory associated with these sacred grounds.

Sometimes, the anticipated emotions can overwhelm you.

However, upon reaching the place where Moghal Masse is laid to rest, I felt an overwhelming sense of emptiness. Yes, there stood a tombstone bearing her name, appearing serene as if it had finally discovered the peace she had yearned for throughout her life—a reunion with her son. While it may sound poetic to read, the true stillness can only be experienced by visiting her grave. We lingered there for a while, contemplating the stark contrast between the two landmarks of her life: the tranquil serenity of the graveyard juxtaposed with the sorrowful cries and creaks emanating from her once-occupied house, burdened with the ache of longing.

The house, a silent sentinel amidst the ebb and flow of life's currents, stands as a stoic witness to the passage of time. Death, with its finality, offers closure—a face and form that we can grasp, a grave that becomes a beacon of remembrance. Yet, what of the loved one who disappears from the living canvas, leaving behind a void that echoes through the corridors of memory? What becomes of the house that becomes a repository of silence, absorbing the whispers of solitude like dust settling on forgotten shelves?

In the quiet corners of this dwelling, where shadows dance with the fading light of day, one can sense the weariness etched into its very bones—a weariness born of years spent holding the weight of absence. Its walls, once vibrant with life's tales, now stand as silent sentinels, bearing witness to the passage of countless seasons. Do we not see the echoes of fatigue etched upon its weathered facade, like the lines of age upon a weathered face?

And yet, amidst this quiet lament, one cannot help but wonder—does the pain of separation linger, seeping into the very essence of the house itself? Do its timbres groan with the weight of unspoken longing, its windows weeping tears of dew in the stillness of the night? Perhaps, in the dead of night, when the world slumbers and dreams take flight, the house whispers secrets to the moon, its creaking walls an echo of silent yearning.

In the depths of its darkness, where shadows dance with the ghosts of memory, the house becomes a vessel for the echoes of the past—a haunting reminder of love's enduring presence, even in absence. And as the night stretches on, and the stars paint patterns upon the sky, one cannot help but feel the house's silent plea—a whispered prayer for a reunion, a longing for the return of those lost to the passage of time.

5

Home Through My Grandmother's Memory

Ayushi Koul

The personal memories of our grandparents have always contributed to the formation of family communicative memory leading to the formation of narrative identities among their children. According to Assmann (2008), this is because the emotional intensity of these memories is far more intense and can create an imprint on a child, providing a foundation for creating personal identity through intergenerational transmission of interpreted past experiences. The landscape of Srinagar city intertwined in the personal memory of my grandmother and that of several others becomes a city within which an abundance of emotions and sensory expressions first evolved. It becomes a space for us where the self, everyday, family and neighbourhood are created. It creates a unity, emotional bond and association with the landscape which has always been distant and in constant flux. The force of this narrative memory has compartmentalised the "good" and the "vicious" creating two separate memory landscapes for our generation. One filled with longing and nostalgia for the past, and the other with the struggling political reality of the region. Through the nostalgic memories of my grandmother this essay explores the abundance of emotions that were experienced in the everyday, creating an intimate bond with the land.

My grandmother was originally from Nai Sarak, Habba Kadal, near the matador station/Tanga adda (horse cart stand). She moved to the neighbourhood of Jogilankar, Rainawari after getting married in her early twenties. Often her conversations dwell on these two neighbourhoods as if Kashmir for her only meant these two spaces. For us born in Delhi, most of our associations with Kashmir are also limited to these specific sites. These two neighbourhoods over the years have become a lens for us to gaze on our unlived past and form a bond with a landscape which could hardly be our home. This fragile bond is not created by visiting or "going back", rather through reiterations of the same personal stories and narratives by our grandparents and parents over thirty years. My grandmother, Phoola Hakim, in remembrance of her late mother, who was lovingly called Jigri, often narrated her daily schedule while living in the neighbourhood.

Jigri would wake up early in the morning to leave home at 3.30 am for Ganpatyar. She would meet other women either on the route or in the temple premises. After their morning darshan of Ganpatyar they would walk for three kilometres to Hari Parbat at Kathi Darwaza where they would sing elaborate hymns and songs to the local goddess perceived to be an avatar of Parvati, consort of Shiva. The morning session of temple strolling would end with going to the Bhairav temple at Gav Kadal. In the evening, she would leave again for a couple of hours to attend evening *aarti* at the ashram of Gopinath Bab, a Kashmiri Shaivite saint. Many such instances ended with conversations over cups of tea readily available either in the temple spaces or enroute at friends' homes. "She also performed many yatras which sometimes took two to three days. She visited religious sites frequently—Tulmul, Zeistha Bagwati, Gangbal, Gosh." My grandmother remembers her mother with utmost affection but she herself struggled, as being the eldest daughter, the responsibility to maintain the household was delegated to her. But Jigri, who had five children, hardly missed these ritual sessions of collective assemblage and singing. Faith did play a significant role in it, but these ordinary ritual practices opened up space for Jigri and many other home-bound women to leave their domestic life behind for a few hours or even days, at an age when there existed no social or technological means to con-nect and socialise with the world. The immediate neighbourhood was the world for most women and relationships formed in and through the neighbourhood became essential in everyday living. The bonds created in these neighbourhoods were maintained by daily meets and greets as well as spontaneous invitations of tea and meals. Jigri, as recalled by my grandmother, would sit at the window of her first-floor room post lunch, overlooking the road leading to Tanga adda which later became Matador stand. There was frequent passing of known faces and recurrent enquires of wellbeing. In several instances, tired workers and travellers were offered meals colloquially termed *"batt"*. Women were invited to share cups of noon chai or kehva over detailed discussions of happenings in their world and emptying their hearts in case of turmoil. Many of these discussions became common knowledge and were transferred from home to home, and sometimes to generations. As my grandmother grew up, it was this common knowledge and structures which governed their lives. It was believed in their neighbourhood that making an invocation at the shrine of Dastageer Saeb could make your wish come true. Therefore, an invocation was made every year for the smooth passing of examinations for all her siblings after which 11 rupees were offered to the shrine. Dastageer Saeb in Khanyar was at a distance from Habba Kadal. After her wedding, my grandmother moved to Rainawari, much closer to Dastageer Saeb and her visits to the shrine became more frequent and her faith stronger. With changes in neighbourhoods post-marriage, places of worship also change, a common transformation in women's lives. Along with Dastageer Saeb, she now often visited Shankracharya and Muqdum Saeb.

With a change in times, women seeking education and becoming part of the workforce in non-agricultural communities, access to the world was easier. The world beyond the neighbourhood opened in my grandmother's life with college. She was a student at Government Women's College, Kothibag, a ten-minute walk from her place. Her group of five girlfriends would assemble at college and quickly escape to the cinema. Their escapes became much more recurrent in the last two years of college as they found a method to navigate the city by themselves, hidden from the eyes of their elders. She recalls this period of travelling from home to cinema halls with a sense of pride. "[The] First film I saw was Taj Mahal, (1963). I watched so many films, even you would not have seen as many." For women, movement has always been restricted. Secret little adventures like watching a film without informing guardians became a means to assert their control over their lives. Navigating the city without familial restrictions and awareness led to a newfound freedom in women's lives which it continues to be.

As a school teacher, she took her students on many picnics, along with her fellow teachers and sometimes even her daughters. The Mughal Gardens were the most frequently visited as they were in the city. My grandmother recalls these trips with relish. The teachers would pack extensive picnic baskets of both cooked and uncooked food. Many times, food was prepared on multiple portable stoves they carried with them; on one of the stoves, a huge amount of rice was always being cooked. Due to social structures and food practices, Kashmiri Pandit women did not eat in a Muslim household, but on such outings, these distinctions did not matter. Picnics created sites where women freed themselves of expectations to maintain the "order" which men would hardly follow. These spaces were no longer marked by religion or any religious practices but moments of joy and enjoyment that everyone contributed to and shared. These were the territories of female staff in which male staff were hardly invited or were completely ignored. Eating the meals together in circles, distributing the food among the students, washing the utensils in nearby water bodies and delegating some responsibility to the students usually brought the day to an end.

Growing up, as these memories were poured into our lives, the imagery of Kashmir became a territory of desire but not that of a sacred landscape, fantasy land, or paradise dwelling on its beauty and nationalistic associations. This desire came from an urge to understand what a life here would have meant in our elders' times. Even though this space in itself is not the same, and has shifted socially, politically and culturally, the nostalgia of the land and the time spent here does not allow generations to leave behind what has been lost.

6

The Pale Pink Walls

Meher Qadri

30-year-old Saba travels the narrow alleys of downtown Srinagar to return home every day. She crosses several barricaded checkpoints wrapped in tangled assortments of concertina wire that branch out like the tense veins running through her body. The camouflage-tainted military structures that have encroached more and more upon the narrow streets of the city go unnoticed by the usual passerby, given how habituated Kashmiris have become with their enforced collective silence. They have become accustomed to navigating through the militarised urban and rural landscape without ever being able to question its emergence after the 1990s insurgency. One such lane she passes through on odd days is lined with a pale pink wall that used to be red at some point, but time and the sun have taken their toll on its colour.

Situated in a residential area, it is just an ordinary wall for the usual commuters on most days.

However, on Fridays, it is flocked by people holding blankets, books and tiffins, with some standing in line with hopeless and desolate looks upon their faces. All of them are waiting outside the heavily guarded gate of the pink wall fortified unevenly with barbed wire along its upper ledge.

The scene is not new to Saba as she crosses this place on Fridays and sometimes remembers getting down from her school bus as a nine-year-old girl in the uptown area of Srinagar. Every morning, she would see scores of people with the same disheartened faces sitting on both sides of the road. For the understanding of a nine-year-old girl, this wasn't something that would leave a mark. But this sight became recurrent in her life in those days of going to and coming back from school. On some days, older women would be substituted by younger women, fathers with brothers, as young brides would show signs of ageing on that roadside wait. However, the uncertainty and the wait on their faces would remain all the same, and in time come to be a marker of a shared despair. To make sense of this daily occurrence, questions arose about who these people were and why they were there each day, which eventually led Saba to the realisation that her school shared its wall with one of the notoriously frequented detention centres of Srinagar City. And that the people she saw waiting every day outside of her school were the family members of the men who had been picked up, had been detained, or had gone missing.

Mothers, grandmothers, fathers, spouses, siblings, children and other close relatives would flock to such detention centres and camps hoping to locate their loved ones. Giving up hope, some would return to their homes after a few days of finding no answers while others would continue this ordeal of waiting for months and years with no answers.

The phone rings and Saba finds herself standing outside the same pale pink wall while a woman keenly glances at her with elderly luminescent eyes. She asks *"tze ti tchuya yeti kahn?"* (Do you also have a loved one [detained] here?) For a moment, Saba feels her tongue frozen, not knowing how to say no. She has been looking for an answer since childhood as to whether the people on the other side of the wall were also a part of those who were beyond its confines. Now she fails at formulating an affirmative answer to the question posed by the elderly woman. All she can come up with is a terse and cordial greeting in her native language— "Salaam."

With shining silver strands in her hair and decades of longing in the lines etched on her face Mogli—the woman in her late sixties—replies *"Waalaikum-as-Salaam koori"* (Peace be upon you, daughter). Saba crouches down on the side of the road to take a place next to her, *"Bas wean tchu oudei geinte, patte tche mein waer"* (Now there's just half an hour left and then it's my turn). As they sit next to one another, Mogli tells her that Aijaz, her 40-year-old son, has been on the other side of this wall and many like it for the last two decades. He had remained missing and unaccounted for after the first few years of a prolonged incarceration. Saba still cannot fully grasp the enormity of the conversation that is about to ensue, finding herself at a loss for words as she sees the woman opening a steel tiffin box. *"Be tchas doori pyethe yiwaan. Awai tchas ye seet tulaan. Aaz soozikh Khoda Seaban cze ti."* (I travel from afar to be here. That is why I pack some food in this tiffin on my way here. Today the Almighty has also brought you here.)

As Mogli takes out a plastic water bottle from a grocery bag and opens it to wash her hands, Saba watches in awe realising that Mogli has been performing this ritual her entire life—like the Muslim ablution ritual of *wuzuu* that is carried out before each of the five daily prayers. The rituals of her religious faith have become intertwined with the rituals of habitual visits to the pink wall, and that too on the holiest day of the week for Muslims.

A small steel tiffin wrapped in a green towel held in Mogli's wrinkled hands glistens as her fingers find their way around the lid. A light aroma of homecooked food escapes the tiffin revealing a reddish potato curry resting on top of some rice.

Artwork by Salman Khursheed

Saba hesitantly asks Mogli about Aijaz. *"Su ous shur. Dukaanas nebre kani tulukh."* (He was a kid. He was apprehended and taken away right outside our vegetable shop.) Aijaz was 18 when he was picked up outside his shop where he would help his father sell groceries. It took Mogli's family 18 months to know of his where-abouts, presuming him to be dead all that while. Aijaz was finally found in Kot Bhalwal jail. Since he was located in Kot Bhalwal, it has been a journey of going back and forth for Mogli and her family over the last 22 years—the charges, a mere suspicion. This is the story of innumerable Kashmiris from the 1990s and even now in 2023 to a lesser degree. One's mere appearance could be a cause for incarceration, detention or simply death given the legal framework established by the State under the garb of anti-insurgency laws like the Disturbed Areas Act (DAA) and Armed Forces Special Powers Act (AFSPA) that facilitate unwarranted detentions without due process throughout the valley. Saba is familiar with this journey from an experience she recalls all too vividly, triggered further by her chance encounter with Mogli. As she recollects, one day while returning from school at the age of 11, she found her home crowded with neighbours and strangers. Amidst the gathered crowd, she located her mother's familiar face—this time pale as that of death. Upon inquiring, she was told that her father, a then-government employee, had left his workplace that afternoon but had not come home as the day turned from the scarlet hues to the greys of the early night. The looming fear and the uncertainty had started to take root as the evening progressed into night.

The men in the family ran in different directions in a city under siege of war to get whatever information they could, while the house remained filled with the hushed wails of the women. This was a common occurrence all over the valley during the 1990s. If the men and the boys left home in the morning for their schools, colleges or work, and did not return by the evening, the presumption of having been killed or picked up by the Indian armed forces was a given. In some unfortunate cases, their whereabouts were never known, sending their families on a never-ending ordeal for decades or till the evidence of their death would end the wait. In the case of those indefinitely marked as the enforced disappeared, such a wait would end with the death of their loved ones who wouldn't stop looking until they themselves passed away. Kashmir has an unexplainable and ironic relationship with death; in some cases, it comes as mercy and in others as an end to hope.

Saba and her family had looked everywhere for five days with unrelenting hope but without any clear hints or answers, until the help from a neighbour's house suddenly came running with unverified news, *"Dapan hez tchiv su tchu SMHS haspatale!"* (It's being said that he has been taken to the SMHS hospital!). Her uncle had jumped up jolted by the abrupt surprise and the promise of hope in trying to understand the messenger, *"Kussu? Kyah tchuk wanaan?"* (Who are you talking about? What are you saying?). *"Showkat Saeb hez ous phone karaan. Dopun yiman dap Majid Saeb tchu SMHSas manz."* (Mr. Showkat was calling over the phone. He said to tell you that Mr. Majid is at the SMHS.)

Bashir, the help, used to work in a neighbouring house that had the only landline connection with a rotary dial phone. They had received a call from the hospital that somebody in one of the wards had recognised Saba's father. They had then proceeded to call the neighbours knowing that people were looking for him. The house erupted in loud cries of joy and the men rushed to the hospital. Saba's father was brought home on a stretcher barely alive and covered in bandages. He was kept under medical care and remained bedridden for the next six months. Every day when Jan Saeb (Mr. Jan), the local nurse, would come to change the bandages, Saba would get a glimpse of the unspeakable torture inflicted on her father's body. This was an 11-year-old's introduction to the horrors of a continued military occupation.

A strange but familiar voice, *"Koori, ratht khyeh cze ti myend ze."* (Daughter, here have a bite or two to eat) pulls an 11-year-old Saba back into her 30-year-old body and she finds Mogli holding a morsel of food close to her mouth. As she takes the first bite of the food, she involuntarily asks *"tuih tchiv kuni zeni aamit?"* (Have you come here alone?). Mogli lets out a faint smile and says, *"Su janatgaar yeetis kaalas ous, aes eaas ikwatai yiwan. Temis gayi wean paanczh wari guzremtis."* (My husband who is in heaven now used to come with me, he passed away five years ago.) Saba takes a breath and closes her eyes for a moment.

Being a heavy smoker, Mogli's husband had died of Chronic Obstructive Pulmonary Disease (COPD) and their only other child, their daughter, was married now. Through such changes in her family life, Mogli had been visiting the detention centre by the pink wall waiting to meet Aijaz religiously every Friday. The harsh bone-chilling Himalayan winters and scorching summers did not deter her from showing up week after week.

The sound of pouring water prompts Saba to open her eyes. Mogli washes her hands and says:

"Asii maajen tche na dagg aasaan. Yane Aijaz Saeb niuukh tane tche mye ze hisse gemit zan. Khaandaar, koor te beyi duniya pak-nawun. Magar akh hisse tchum emsi Aijazas seet. Mei tche akh zang gari gandith te byaakh bare nebar. Shikmas manz tchum naa rotchmut. Mye tche aasaan ajeeb dagg paanas. Zan tchim yead shrake waalaan. Wumrah geyem nendir ker mitis. Dapaan tchina Aeshiq gov maaji kun pothur marun, so hai zol kari te kahey."

(We mothers feel a special type of pain for our children. Since Aijaz was taken it feels as if I've been split in half. I've had to carry forth with my husband, my daughter and this world without him. But that other half of me is always with Aijaz. One of my legs is tied to my domestic life and the other to all these public places that I have to visit to meet him. I've carried him in my womb and raised him. I feel an ache in my body for him. It's been ages since I've slept properly. As they say, true love is that of a mother and her child and the mother who loses her only child, how can she ever find sleep?)

Saba almost chokes on her breath upon hearing this from Mogli and thinks of all the mothers of Kashmir whose sons were killed or have been disappeared, never to be found again. The separation and longing are insufferable but a strange condition that connects all these women is their faith in Allah, and it eases their journey. Some mothers have died while waiting to know if their sons were alive and some have died in the hope to meet them in the here-after. Noticing Saba's moist eyes, Mogli puts her arm around the young woman.

"Khodah tchu raheem, su kari sahal. Maa aas dil haaraan." (God is gracious, He will ease our struggle. Do not be disheartened.) As the sentry calls Mogli's name, Saba is still trying to fathom how a woman who has gone through so much is able to give her strength and consolation. Unwilling for this encounter to end, Saba helps Mogli up and offers to carry her bags inside till the checkpoint, which is where they scrutinise who gets to go into the military compound and who must wait outside. *"Adsa pakh."* (Alright, let's go,) Mogli smiles with an unsettling calm. As they start walking towards the entrance, Saba feels her feet getting heavier with

every step that she takes. What does it mean to walk into a garrison? How does it feel to be inside those militarised walls? Although Saba has lived all her life in a heavily-guarded open-air prison—the Kashmir Valley, the most militarised zone in the world—this is her first time walking into a jail within that larger jail.

How does freedom change beyond these walls and where does it find refuge? Saba makes this short journey accompanying Mogli to the checkpoint as her heart gets heavier by the minute. With the air around her thickening with each breath, the noises from outside are muting themselves out. Is it just her or does everyone else feel like this inside these walls?

As they reach the checkpoint and Mogli and her belongings are put through a process of frisking and inspection, Saba bids goodbye to the woman she had not thought she would meet when her day had started. A woman who reminds her of so many mothers of Kashmir. A woman whose bravery in the face of adversity could light up a thousand and one dark nights of waiting. As Saba bids Mogli goodbye, she leans in for a longer hug than she had expected, as if their wombs have aligned and were conversing one last time.

As Saba turns around to make that walk back from inside the pale pink wall towards the world where military occupation has been normalised, she remembers a few lines from Anna Akhmatova's poem *Requiem* that she had read just last week:

> *I have learned how faces fall,*
>
> *How terror can escape from lowered eyes,*
>
> *How suffering can etch cruel pages*
>
> *Of cuneiform-like marks upon the cheeks.*
>
> *I know how dark or ash-blond strands of hair*
>
> *Can suddenly turn white. I've learned to recognise*
>
> *The fading smiles upon submissive lips,*
>
> *The trembling fear inside a hollow laugh.*
>
> *That's why I pray not for myself*
>
> *But all of you who stood there with me*
>
> *Through fiercest cold and scorching July heat*
>
> *Under a towering, completely blind red wall.*

The guard rushes Saba to leave by blowing his authoritative whistle as her soul ails to remain by the elderly woman's side. The lines of Akhmatova's poem reverberate through her mind as the gate closes behind her. She turns around, looks back, and mumbles "completely blind pale pink wall."

7

Celebration of the Present, Mourning the Past, Yearning for the Future

Ayushi Koul

This particular essay is a means to understand and complicate the return of the Kashmiri Pandit community to their homeland for the annual celebration of Zeth Athem using autoethnographic and ethnographic methods used by Ruth Behar in her book *The Vulnerable Observer*. This analysis is futher built by using the work of Tracy Davis (2010), Maurice Halbswachs (1950) and Joseph Roach (1996). For the Kashmiri Pandit community, the celebration of Zed Athem is haunted by the events of 1989. This haunting or as Davis calls, citationality, becomes an aspect of performative time. This essay also studies the festival of Zed Athem by drawing attention to the community's association with land and the cultural-religious changes under Dogra rule.

Artwork by Shajar Lateef

In June 2021, my aunt made a last-minute plan to attend Zed Athem as flight restrictions due to the pandemic were lifted. Zed Athem is an annual festival celebrated on the birthday of Goddess Raginya at her only shrine Kheer Bawani in Tulmul, Ganderbal, Kashmir. According to the Hindu Calendar, this day falls on the eighth day of Jyeshta month or the third month. I, my aunt, her daughter and our grandmother took an early flight the next day to reach Kashmir which approximately takes one hour and thirty minutes. Before leaving the airport, we were stopped to show the RTPCR report. One among the many officials who were appointed on COVID duty, came to guide us personally saying, "*Tuhiv chu na aamit Bod Doh Khatr, as chu gasan dil khush tohiv vashit, Kashir chi ni ruzmut su kashir wyen.*" (You are surely here for the big day, my heart is filled with happiness when I see you. Kashmir is not that Kashmir now.) Blessings were passed as we left saying Khuda Hafiz. One might think how he recognised us but Kashmiri Pandit women are easier to recognise because of their pierced inner ears. Centuries of co-existence has also taught people to recognise each other. After leaving Srinagar airport, we took a cab to Ganderbal. The route crossed Srinagar, which had been home to my family for generations. On the entire journey, my aunt and grandmother were recalling and telling us which route reached which destination. On certain instances they would discuss which prominent shop used to be highlight of the road or which family lived on which road. In one of the instances, my aunt got excited and said, "This used to be my bus stop when I was in New Era (School)." The driver, a young Kashmiri Muslim reciprocated and also added details that had come to pass in the recent past "This is a new highway, it goes directly to Ganderbal," he mentioned. "That is why I couldn't recognise it," said Grandmother. Conversations flowed from what was and what is with some silent patches till we reached Tulamul. Most of the conversation for grandmother ended with "*Soori gov pat tabha,*" meaning "everything was destroyed after."

Tracy Davis, while describing Theatrical time, discusses the words of the Chief of the Native American Tribe Crow Nation or Absaroka. She writes: Plenty Coup said, "After this nothing happened"; Davis uses this to define Theatrical Time as after the Theatrical event, nothing else can be added to it. One can remember it but not add to it. Similar words are used by the Kashmiri population to describe the year 1990, "*Soori gov tabha.*" Older generations of Kashmiris see the year 1989, marked by the rise of militancy and brutal counteraction by the Indian forces as the one leading to the fall of the region and the end of peace. Massacres, killings, and rape became everyday news. The culture of violence and chaos took over. But unlike what Plenty Coup said, for Kashmiris, everything did not end. On the contrary, the event became a citation.

The threat of being a religious minority forced Kashmiri Pandits to leave their homeland amid conflict after some prominent members of the community were killed. Mass migration of the community or the exodus has since become a citation for the community. Davis sees such citationality as an aspect of Performative time which percolates and haunts through tangible or intangible memory. For my aunt and grandmother, roads, bus stops and the surrounding buildings became the medium of taking them into the past, while being in the present. According to Davis "Performative time is a distinct way to account for people's location in history. It allows for nonlinearity, or nonseriality as a factor in perception as well as the teleology of time's asynchronicity, polychronicity, and achronism, overturning a straightforward concept of temporal succession."

Since the rise of conflict, the Kheer Bawani temple compound has been surrounded by the army, their barbed wires and bunkers. There was perhaps some news or rumour that militants were planning to bomb the temple. No temple has ever been burned down in Kashmir. Davis mentions that heritage sites become a medium of creating a future identity. Similarly, the presence of the Indian Army "protecting" the Hindu religious site from a blast that might happen in the future was done with the intention of having better relations with Kashmiri Pandits. In the words of Davis, "they lay claim to a version of the future being present in the here-and-now of visitors' experience." A "future" blast in the temple since 1990 which has led to the entire temple space being filled with troops of the Indian army never allows Kashmiris, both local and migrated, to forget the rise of conflict. Their presence, for my aunt and grandmother, is a marker of the new world they were forced into. On every visit to Kheer Bawani, I remember seeing men with their guns, bunkers and barbed wires.

I have crossed the path surrounded by barbed wires and armed men several times, even though I never lived through my family's past. But the past that is the exodus and rise of conflict has become such a strong citation that there was never a question of not knowing about it. The past always lived in my present of visiting the region, and would continue to live in the future.

Under the gaze of armed men, there exist things in the Kheer Bawani temple which have no relationship with the conflict. Some consider the many maple trees surrounding the compound to be thousands of years old. There is a stream in which it is mandatory to bathe before entering the temple premise. There are three miniature temples in front of the Nag or holy spring which people worship. Generations have witnessed their being there. They became a tangible memory of the past before conflict broke out in the region. They were present in our past, present and probable future. Maurice Halbswachs (1950), in his chapter "Space and The Collective Memory", discusses the association of the group with their surroundings. According to him, space and humans both influence and evolve each other. A group leaves its imprints on the space and surroundings which, in turn, affect the practices that people adapt into everyday routines or religious ritual practices. In his words, "The group not only transforms the space into which it has been inserted, but also yields and adapts to its physical surroundings. It becomes enclosed within the framework it has built." In discussing the association of religion and land, Halbwachs mentions that "religions are rooted in the land." In Kashmir, the two dominant religions, Hinduism and Islam, leave their imprints on every corner of the region. Zutshi (2014) in her work *Kashmir's Contested Past* discusses the varied historical narratives written around/on Kashmir constructing Kashmir as a holy site. By shedding light on the religious and sacred texts written on Kashmir, she dwells on how these texts have highlighted Kashmir as a sacred space of both Hinduism and Islam. [8]

---

8 The literary landscape of Kashmir can be dated back to the 8th-century texts *Rajatarangini* and *Nilamata Purana* before the Islamic acculturation. Citing M. Stein's translation and memoir on *Rajatarangini* which also focuses on the landscape of the valley, Zutshi writes, "Landscape itself becomes a historical

Interestingly in Kashmiri, springs are called Nags, possibly drawing on Naga myths. It remains a mystery what Nagas signify: whether they can be perceived as a community of people, snakes or deities. In the cultural memory of locals, these are powerful beings which if unhappy can cause havoc in the valley.[9] Religious transitions could also not decrease the importance of Nagas in the valley; rather both Buddhist and Islamic traditions incorporated them in their cultural narratives. According to Shonaleeka Kaul (2018), "Fluid, changeable, ubiquitous, yet revered, the nagas were classic myth-builders. This is especially relevant to the way stories woven around nagas and enacted through their physical and moral agency construct the 'imagined landscape' of Kashmir." M.A. Wani also notes that the beliefs related to Naga worship were such that Rishis and Sufis considered the springs sacred and their spirits personifying humans and snakes.[10]

---

document within which the past was preserved and from which it could be retrieved—a sort of archive." [2014, pp. 217]

In the context of Kashmir, forest and spring become an essential part of Kashmir's literary landscape, including floods, famine and other natural calamities, both in literary texts as well as cultural memory. Here it is essential to discuss Shonaleeka Kaul (2018) who unlike Zutshi specifically looks at one text. It becomes essential to talk about her work because its subject *Rajatarangini* is a much older text. Kaul discusses a literary tradition in Sanskrit Kavya by Kalhana which constructs the region as homeland and sacred geography. In the chapter "Imagined landscape— Myth, Memory and Place-making", Kaul explores the role of place making with reference to the physical features of the land upheld in the narrative text *Rajatarangini* which then travels via local folklore and memory

9 One such havoc associated with Nagas are floods, which is a recurring theme in texts like *Rajatarangini*. These floods also relate to the political narratives by Kalhana to discuss how rulers dealt with the situation while continuing with practices to keep the deities/Nagas content. Other calamities said to be caused by Nagas are untimely snowfall and rain destroying the harvest, leading to famine. In one of the narratives in *Rajatarangini*, discussed by Kaul, Nagas were personified as thieves. Moreover sculptures of Nagas could also be found on ancient dams, possibly for providing protection from their wrath.

10 Interestingly, Wani and many other scholars mention narratives as per which Nagas were claimed to be converted by the Sufi saints and scholars. One such popular text is *Dastur-us-Salikin* (1554–55) written by Baba Daud Khaki on the life of his *murshid*, Shaykh Hamza. As per Khaki, the text is written after being in close contact with Shaykh Hamza, where he has been eye witness to

The space having its effect on the people allowed them to create ritualistic practices incorporating the space. A bath in the stream before entering the temple, the worship of the Nag/spring, and then parikrama or circumambulating the spring have become important practices of worship in Kashmiri Pandit culture. The spring, if not the idol, which was later consecrated, is revered by all communities. It is believed that the colour of the water changes according to the situation in Kashmir. During the peak of violence in the 1990s, the water turned dark and remained so for a long time. The locals belonging to all communities do not enter the temple compound after consuming eggs or any form of meat. It can displease the Nagas and cause havoc for the people.

To not upset the Nagas and also to her past, my grandmother, who left her homeland in her 50s now aged 87, and suffering from Osteoporosis, bathed in the cold stream twice before entering the main compound. "It is a ritual; it has to be done" was her argument when she was confronted by us. Having a bath in the early morning allowed her to relive the past which made her forget her present health condition. When the pain struck, she said "I know I shouldn't have but I have always taken a bath before entering since I was a little girl." The memory of the ritual practices performed including the bath in the cold water is the intangible memory of life before she had to leave her homeland. For us, it was a mere ritual which could be skipped, but for her following all the ritual practices and norms allowed her past to intersect with the present. Similarly, participating in this annual festival as well as being in that space allows people to revisit the past and live the future in which they have returned to their homeland.

Tired from the travel, I sat down under the closest maple tree beside the Nag where an elderly couple were already seated. They offered me kehva and the elderly man initiated a conversation. Are you from Jammu or Delhi. Delhi, I said. Where was home?

---

events. The text is said to be blessed by Hamza which provides authenticity which cannot be questioned. *Dastur-us-Salikin* presents the many miracles of Hamza by comparing him to Prophet Issa for his ability to cure the sick and return the sight of the blind.

Rainawari. What is your Grandfather's name? M.K. Wanchoo. He used to work in the Accountants General office, he stated. I cannot say I was stunned at how quickly he could locate my family. This is because of the closely knit community system and endogamy practised in various districts of Kashmir, especially Srinagar.[11] He introduced himself as Ashok Toshkhani, who was my grandfather's colleague. He also happened to know some other members of my family. Like some Kashmiri Pandit families, Toshkhani Saeb chose to stay in Kashmir after the violence began. Presently, he lives in Rajbagh, Srinagar, with his wife; his children are settled in some western country. I enquired how his life has been and why he stayed back. For Toshkhani Saeb, living in his motherland was more important. He also never directly received any threat from anyone throughout his life in the region. Even though he had migrated during the peak of militancy, he soon went back after a few days. We exchanged phone numbers as he wanted to contact my grandfather. Toshkhani Saeb and his wife are among the eight hundred families that chose to live in Kashmir when thousands were migrating to safety. Many people, especially right-wing Indians who often question "What about Kashmiri Pandits?" choose to ignore the narratives of these eight hundred families and their lives in the region. Many of the non-migrated Kashmiri Pandits have complained of becoming invisibilised by the State after the abrogation of Article 370. [12]

11 Kashmir had/has a great rural/urban divide. Srinagar and its residents take much pride in being sophisticated in language, education and other cultural and trade activities.

12 Sanjay Tickoo, president of Kashmiri Pandits Sangharsh Samiti in a press release writes "Survival of Non-Migrant Kashmiri Pandits/Kashmiri Hindus is right now at stake in Kashmir Valley which can lead to chaos and starvation and even psychology issues and in worst cases, deaths among the left out 808 families because some persons in the bureaucracy are showing cold shoulders towards the leftover community for the reasons best known to them since July 2018 till today. Since the 5th of August, 2019 there is a huge vacuum between general public with those bureaucrats who are in decision-making body in the UT of J&K, and left out Kashmiri Pandit/Kashmiri Hindus are worst sufferers of this vacuum which creates un-necessary hurdles in survival to the leftover community and the reasons behind this vacuum are unknown to all. It may be apt to mention here that despite recommendations issued by the Ministry of Home Affairs and consecutive

Unlike families that underwent exodus, non-migrated Kashmiri Pandit families have witnessed and have become part of the changing landscape of Kashmir. They have lived through several curfews, internet blockage, and army checkpoints which have all made their social and political identities distinct from that of the migrated Pandit families. Their presence in the valley has constructed these identities, unlike the past which has constructed mine or my grandmother's identity. Toskhani Saeb might have been able to visit the Kheer Bawani temple every month or week but he has also lived through a month-long curfew and complete network blockage.

directions from Hon'ble High Court of Jammu and Kashmir supported with reports submitted by two Parliamentary Standing Committees and other likewise recommendations from different offices in favor of left out Kashmiri Pandits/Kashmiri Hindus living in Kashmir Valley are put in dust bins in order to achieve some hidden agenda against for staying back in Kashmir Valley. The irony is that these officers/officials are using their bureaucratic and clerical skills to manipulate the facts to keep their superiors in dark in order to hide their incompetency and manipulative practices particularly in the Department of Disaster Management Relief, Rehabilitation and Reconstruction and are playing with the lives of 808 left out Kashmiri Pandit/Kashmiri Hindu families. The left out Kashmiri Pandit/Kashmiri Hindu families are made to suffer even after clear recommendation(s) from Central Government and directions from Hon'ble High Court. It may be also worth to mention here that Ministry of Home Affairs issued recommendations in the year 2015 and later on Hon'ble High Court passed directions in the year 2016 in favor of left out Kashmiri Pandits but we made to suffer because some officers/officials of the local government do not tolerate our presence in Kashmir Valley as such are pushing us towards the wall and we are forced to choose extreme steps like sitting on fast-unto-death. "(https://cjp.org.in/non-migrant-kashmiri-pandits-hold-protest-march-in-srinagar/)."

Artwork by Shajar Lateef

3

Yaarbal

8

Bayt-ul-Huzn: The House of Sorrows

Khateeba Syed

"In this city, I am memory."

—Elie Wiesel

Photograph by Khateeba Syed

While wandering through the old lanes of Fateh Kadal in downtown Kashmir, a place where the inexorable forces of history and modernity collide and every lane whispers the riddles of the past. Shahida's gaze is drawn to a half-burned *wuroosi*[13] precariously clinging to the window of a *Zoon Deb*[14] of an Old House, which seems to yearn for rescue, silently beseeching the passerby to mend its broken spirit. As if a soul pleading

---

13 Traditional wooden shutters, often ornamental, used as partition walls in Kashmiri homes. These shutters can be rolled up or down from hanging grooves in the ceiling to create separate areas within a room. The term "Wuroosi" is believed to be of Persian origin, "uroosi" meaning "hidden bride", and these shutters are known for their ability to absorb and withstand seismic shocks.

14 A cantilevered balcony designed for moon viewing.

for salvation, meanwhile warning the passerby to not commit the sin of forgetting. Its frayed edges and charred scars serve as a poignant reminder of Shahida's own long-lost childhood days when the smell of freshly baked *lavasa* (traditional thin unleavened flat bread) filled the air and innocence reigned, those were the times when she and her siblings revelled in games upon the *Tak* of wuroosi—a nook within their *dewankhan*, a vast hall in traditional Kashmiri houses where guests and family gatherings flourished. Now, the city bore witness to numerous such hollowed houses like a rib without a heart, that had once echoed with endless memories.

Ah Memory! Memory like an ethereal aura, carries a scent that clings eternally to one's soul. It is something indescribable, transcending words—a sentiment akin to the fragrance of the old lantern her mother would light during the prolonged *waeyr* (power cuts) in their mohalla. Those memories resurfaced, vividly portraying the everyday struggles and the hidden anxieties that veiled the women of her household. But, is memory a blessing or a curse? Could it still be a memory if it was forgotten? Might the act of forgetting serve as a tool to reconstruct what had been lost? Pondering these questions, Shahida ventures through the winding lanes witnessing the city's buildings, once custodians of a generation's tales, now standing as silent witnesses to the relentless march of urbanisation. Traditional curbstones lay shattered along the boulevard road, ruthlessly uprooted and vandalised under the banner of "Remaking of City". The city's narrative was being rewritten, our histories were either denied or grotesquely distorted.

Amidst this complex urban metamorphosis, Shahida believes that some stories endured while others faded, like footprints in the shifting sands of time. Stories of women from less privileged backgrounds languished in obscurity, their voices overshadowed by the grand narratives. Women like her grandmother—steeped in folk culture—held a lot of innocence. They wielded their agency, engaged in political acts through culturally diverse practices, and were the authors of their own destinies. Yet, they remained forgotten, their existence fading into oblivion, much like the mulberry tree (*tul kul*) that clings resolutely to a crevice in the concrete walls of her ancestral home. Once a bearer of fruit, now stood barren—a living witness like her name, *"Shahida"*, the witness—

to the gradual erosion of memories that no longer conform to their newly established urban identities. Her eyes witnessed the turquoise walls cracking, mohallas undergoing rapid gentrification, and the rapidly changing urban panorama casting off the collective memories of the *yaarbal kakins*—women who claimed their spaces in their own way, gathered at watering places to discuss the mundane aspects of life. These water bodies, endowed with a history of solace, perhaps owing to their inherent connection with water, bore witness to the spectrum of hues of their *pherans*[15] and the tales etched beneath the corner of their eyes. Shahida believes that the water safeguards their secrets and silently guards their collective memories, moulding the very essence of the city. Meanwhile, a cracked voice emerges amid this silence surrounding the vandalised stairs of Jehlum, *"Ye yaarbal chu waen yateem, te yateemas ku wade,"* the voice of Azeez Maas, lone surviving neighbour from days gone by, laments. "This yaarbal is an orphan now, and who mourns an orphan?" she muses. Who grieves for what is forgotten? Azeez Maas along with the other women in the vicinity, used to venture out together; it's been ages now, and the yaarbal is now an unrecognisable sight. The aged stairs that led to the water, where women congregated, now lie in ruins, the entire layout has transformed, rendering women unwelcome.

Seeking solace for her tumultuous mind, which mirrors the city's chaos, Shahida arrives at the entrance of an ancient Sufi shrine, enclosed by a wooden railing fence. *Deajh* (votive rags) of varying colours and fabrics, each unique and unmatched, are tightly knotted together—a tapestry of faith, collective suffering, and hope. These knots, connected to each other like the spine of an old woman, conceal truths beneath their layers. A young woman in traditional attire approaches the railing, bearing a shining steel bangle, and adds it to the existing chain of knots. The moment the knot is tied, it transforms into an everlasting bond, bridging the realms of the seen and unseen, hope and despair. Prominently suspended at the heart of the shrine, a green signboard bears the stern declaration, *"Mastoorat ka aana manna hai,"* translating to

---

15 Traditional long, loose dress worn by people of Kashmir, especially during winters.

"Entry for Women Prohibited." Qadri Sob, the shrine's devoted guardian, staunchly enforces this prohibition, citing it as "inauspicious" and a sin for women to transgress this sacred threshold. But does such concern for women truly signify benevolent control over them?

A group of women assemble within the shrine's adjoining courtyard, each contributing her unique presence and purpose. Some carried bundles of fresh vegetables and aromatic spices, while others engaged in animated conversations. A few whispered prayers softly, their fingers gently tracing the beads of a rosary as they immersed themselves in the meditative practice of *zikr* (recitation of attributes of Allah). Meanwhile, others find solace in simply resting comfortably, their legs stretched out, without any imposed guilt, unburdened by societal expectations.

This space transcends the confines of public and private, liberating them from the confines of their prescribed gender roles, and emerges as a "third space" for these women—a sanctuary where women redefine norms and reclaim their freedom and individuality amid their mundane acts. Shahida gazes upon their reflections in the shrine's stained-glass windows, symbolising their presence and the paradox of their invisibility.

Shahida deftly traverses the patriarchal dominance that has long existed in public spaces. Raj Maas, a fisherwoman with her catch of lifeless silver gleaming on the pavement, is one of the women who stride with unwavering confidence. Often unfairly stereotyped as "violent", they adamantly reject the role of passive spectators in their own stories. The streets are their battlegrounds, and their agency demonstrates their resilience.

However, the historic downtown streets hold more than just personal stories. They bear the weight of collective memories and cultural identities that have been eroded by urbanisation's brutal force. The demands of progress have shrouded the essence of what was. Nonetheless, women persist in asserting their presence. Their footsteps proclaim that these streets belong to them as much as anyone else. The narrative of downtown Kashmir, though rewritten and sometimes denied, can never obliterate the stories carved into the very stones of its buildings. Ghettoisation and class politics attempt to stereotype the people of these overcrowded spaces, yet the women continue to resist, forging paths of agency through the intricate threads of paradoxes. The city may change, but the women who traverse its streets, cradling its history in their gaze and hopes in their hearts, remain as steadfast as the eternal flow of the Jehlum.

9

Gender, Leisure and the Public Sacred Spaces of Srinagar City

Muntaha Amin

On a pleasant sunny day in August this year, I, along with some of my friends, decided to go to the Hazratbal Dargah. We entered the premises in the late afternoon. As I made my way to the Dargah, I couldn't help but notice a bustling marketplace filled with tempting street food stalls, an enchanting wicker shop displaying different kinds of planters and shelves, hanging lighting fixtures, enticing jewellery shops, and shops displaying beautiful papier mache artworks like paintings, boxes and picture frames.

I watched as my friend Sadaf purchased a photo frame in white and pastel green hues from one of the papier mache stores for her cousin's birthday. As we entered the Dargah, I observed an atmosphere akin to a lively community fair. Young people browsed through book stalls while children played around. A newlywed couple in their wedding attire strolled by, while college girls sat near the Dal enjoying each other's company. Families gathered on picnic sheets, savouring cups of chai or kehva.

Inside the masjid complex, we offered the afternoon namaz. The women's cabin was cramped with relatively less space than the men's. Kids were playing hide and seek at the exterior end of the woman's prayer cabin.

I have always been intrigued by women's leisure, particularly outside of traditional domestic environments. I often wonder what this looks like in rural or semi-urban areas with conservative values. In Kashmir, I observe men engaging in various recreational activities such as playing sports in playgrounds, cricket matches on the streets or in Eid-gahs or *Aads* (stony riversides). They also enjoy card games in picturesque locations. We see them cycling, taking long evening drives, visiting barbecue shops at night, and frequenting cafes and restaurants late in the evenings.

Artwork by Shajar Lateef

Even within the confines of their homes, older women have become accustomed to associating leisure with simple tasks performed in groups (such as cutting vegetables and doing household chores), engaging in gossip, and enjoying a nap under the sun. On the other hand, younger women may dress up for special occasions like Eid only to find themselves participating in photoshoots with cousins after completing tiring domestic duties related to meal preparation, serving guests, and cleaning. While public spaces offer opportunities for women to partake in activities such as picnics, these outings often involve male "guardians" or family members.

There often isn't privacy, freedom of thought, action, self-discovery, independence and expression of vulnerability in such "guarded" outings. I am working on a film on gender and public spaces. During my recent location scouting trip, I had the opportunity to explore various public areas in Srinagar, including visits to dargahs and shrines. These experiences provided valuable insights into women's presence and experiences within these spaces. In University, in a conversation with a friend Sajida (a woman living in Srinagar city), I was told: "In religious gatherings in our mohalla, women discuss different societal issues. Parents in fact encourage young women to join these spaces."

While in Srinagar, I observed that holy sites such as dargahs and Khanqahs serve not only as places of worship but also as social gathering spots for women. These spaces provide opportunities for conversation, emotional release, leisurely strolls, or even simple picnics outside the confines of their homes.

Shrines offer intriguing glimpses into the public life of the city. Dargahs, in particular, are often accompanied by bustling markets and attractive street food stalls. Women freely visit these sacred places without any societal or familial restrictions, as they are considered religious spaces. As a result, these become unconventional areas for leisurely walks and enjoyable picnics for some women. In Kashmir, many shrines are typically located on hills with awe-inspiring views of lakes and rivers, creating a sense of being at a picnic spot. Therefore, the interaction of gender in these public spaces provides one with interesting insights.

During my visit to the Dargah this summer, I had the chance to engage in a brief conversation with some women. Sumaya's family was enjoying their nunchai session, creating an atmosphere reminiscent of a picnic. A kettle served hot chai while wicker baskets overflowed with *kulche* and *czott* (traditional Kashmiri bread). The children gleefully played together, chasing each other around. Sumaya mentioned that they frequently visit the Dargah in the evenings for prayer, followed by a leisurely exploration and tea time.

Two young girls wearing backpacks sat facing the other side of the Dal. They told me they had just come from college to roam around for a bit. On occasion, they visit eateries nearby, and visit street vendors selling jewellery or other items in the outdoor market.

A newly-wed bride, still wearing clothes from her trousseau, was there with her husband. She said they thought they should come to the Dargah for some alone time and to seek blessings from the sacred space after their marriage.

In the women's prayer cabin, Asiya was sitting and waiting for the prayer call with her infant. Her friends were playing with her infant who kept giggling. A security guard came to shut the door of the women's cabin as prayer time was nearing. Asiya and her friend took turns holding the infant as they prayed.

An old woman kept doing zikr on her *tasbeeh* (rosary) and seemed in a state of utmost concentration and meditation with her God. Women are often seen offering *taehar* (Kashmiri turmeric rice-serving) in shrine compounds, sometimes coming to clean them or offering other services.

I witnessed a group of middle-aged women in the Khanqah discussing the challenges they encounter within their households. They supported one another by offering empathy, guidance, and consolation as needed.

In these trips to the shrine-spaces in Srinagar, I saw how shrines offer some liminal spaces of leisure outside the homes for women. These are spaces in the inbetweenness between public and private, between allowed and restricted, between sacred and mundane.

Public sacred spaces serve as diverse platforms of agency within religious and cultural systems for Muslim women by being places of worship, catharsis, intimate prayer as well as a space for assembly, communion, sharing festivities, food, vulnerabilities as well as happiness and wish fulfilment. In some Muslim-populated countries in South Asia and Europe, Masjids also offer spaces of communion, learning and teaching religious scriptures, history and values amongst groups of women in secluded spaces.[16] They function not only as recreational areas but also as therapeutic environments conducive to conversations with God and fellow women. By offering a shift in mindset, fostering emotional connections, empowering the navigation of patriarchal norms, and providing an alternative space beyond the confines of home, these spaces feel like agents that might be contributing to navigating the mental well-being of women in traditional societal set-ups.

16 Mazumdar, Shampa, and Sanjoy Mazumdar. 2001. "Rethinking public and private space: Religion and women in Muslim society." Journal of Architectural and Planning Research 18, no. 4 (December 2001): 302–324.

10

Alam Sahib Shrine: A Symbol of the Spiritual and a Conversation with Jiji

Sadaf Masoodi

On a chilly November afternoon, *Mahjabeena* sits with her arms inside her *tille*[17]-embroidered pheran, holding a *kanger,*[18] in the *baithak* (living room) of her parents' home, which faces the Alam Sahib shrine. She starts treading down memory lane. On being asked about the past, she begins with a sigh that escapes her lips like a cloud in the cold air.

Sadaf's Jiji looking over the Alam Sahib shrine; photograph by Sadaf Masoodi.

17 Traditional embroidery done with threads on fabric in Kashmir.
18 Earthen fire-pot lit with coal and ashes, used in Kashmir for warmth during winters.

She laments in retrospection, the "waning faith" in the religious symbolism. She grew up and "witnessed miracles" in a tradition that many from following generations discard as "ignorance-in-belief". Alam Sahib to her symbolises that "fading-with-time" spiritual conviction.

In the continuous battle of trying to fit native realities in modern philosophies, which deep down almost always feel alien, I sat with my 70-year-old aunt, dearly called Jiji, to tread on the memory map of a tradition-of-faith, of a place that shaped us and our perspectives on the spiritual and political—Jiji's and mine.

Just like Jiji, being born in the lap of a shrine, Alam Sahib in Srinagar city's downtown area, both of our generations witnessed the tumult of decades of conflict.

A tradition that originates from the profundity of Sufi philosophy embraced people of Jiji's generation in the worst of their political and personal times—the embrace that I witnessed waning in my generation. My aunt and I both ponder over this embrace of the spiritual.

As her parents' and my grandparents' home stands close to the shrine, Jiji has a history of memory associated with the place. She recalls the dirges of the distressed who would come and visit the shrine and vent their grief aloud in this safe space during turbulent times.

"Post-militancy period in 1990s, it was difficult to commute to places including shrines, but occasionally even then, I would hear women's wails from inside the shrine. It was that wailing in this space of Imam Hussein[19] during militancy was their therapy."

19 Grandson of Prophet Muhammad, who was martyred on 10th Muharram, also known as Ashura.

Interior and exterior views of the Alam Sahib shrine; Photographs by Sadaf Masoodi.

Alam Sahib shrine enshrines various relics of Prophet Muhammad's family (Peace be upon them), that include relics from Karbala, Iraq, where the Prophet's grandson Imam Hussein was martyred during Muharram, the first month of the Islamic calendar. It is noted in various historical accounts that the relics were brought by a saint, Mir Syyed Ahmad Kirmani. These sacred artefacts include a shawl of the Prophet's daughter, Fatima, the bloodstained clothes of Imam Hussein, blessed shoes and a flag of the Prophet. Some of the artefacts are displayed every year during the month of Muharram. Devotees from all around Kashmir come to offer salutations to the Prophet's family as they gaze upon these sacred belongings of the Prophet and his family.

While some of these relics are displayed to the people during Muharram, few of them are never shown. Locals believe that these were handed to the saint who brought them to the shrine on this strict condition, that some of the relics must never be taken out from the *pitara* (box).

Legend has it, that some people who curiously attempted to open the box immediately met with tragedies on account of the "sacrilege".

"I have heard from my elders that once a man attempted to open the pitara. As he opened its lid, a cloth-roll started winding off; he kept unwinding it, for what seemed like hours and yet the cloth-roll wouldn't end for him to be able to see what was inside. He was shaken with fear, realising he might have desecrated the relics. Throwing all the cloth back inside the pitara, closing it again, he did his *tauba* (repentance) then and there, for the act."

In another such incident as narrated by the residents around the shrine, another man who attempted to open the box fell sick and just a few days after, passed away.

"I am a witness to this incident as a child: once a storm hit the surrounding areas and there was a giant *chinar*[20] adjacent to the shrine, one branch of which fell on a house near the shrine and it crushed the roof and walls of the house, while one part of the trunk fell on the shrine and damaged nothing of the building made of mud and bricks."

People associated with the place witnessed miracles in it and such incidents are abundant. From the turbulent times after the armed uprising in Kashmir against India, bodies of some militants, shot by the Indian army were laid on the stairs of the shrine.

---

20 Huge deciduous trees found in Kashmir.

People testify to the strong spiritual forces inside the shrine, even in the period when every place in Kashmir was deserted.

"During the armed uprising in Kashmir, there was a curfew once and the Indian armed personnel came to ask for the keys from the guardian of the shrine, who also resides here, to conduct their search inside the shrine. He gave them the keys and we watched them enter the shrine, peeking through our windows and doors. Every living person in the neighbourhood is witness to this incident; when they came out of the shrine, they were struck by fear. Something prevented them from touching the box in which the relics are kept. They shook their heads in fear and shock and left the shrine, saying to their officer *'Sahib yahan andar se koi mera haath pakad raha hai'* (Sir, there is something holding my hand inside)."

It is also related in various narrations about the miracles associated with the shrine, that any time someone tried to take the pitara from its place, strange things happened, as witnessed by older people of the vicinity.

"My elders recall a story that once a famine hit Kashmir; people decided to take relics out from different shrines across the valley to assemble them at one place and then pray to Allah. They assembled near the shrine in the historic Eidgah. When they took out the relics from this shrine, a storm hit the place and the sky turned red. Many elders read this as a warning sign and let relics of Alam Sahib shrine be untouched."

Jiji recalls that some decades ago, custodians of the shrine were renovating it and while some renovation work had to happen inside the sanctum, strong storms hit the place. The custodians made sure to be extra careful with the relics inside the box while renovating the shrine.

Alam Sahib for Jiji is a symbol of miracles that she witnessed in her personal life as well. A cancer survivor, during her battle with the disease, the Alam Sahib shrine became a motif of her dreams, that would calm her distress. She was convinced that her time in the world was over, but when she recalled some dreams where she would be in and around the shrine, it would give her inexplicable respite during that time of distress.

"Once I saw myself inside the compound of the shrine and a staircase going up to the sky through the shrine. I saw there was *noor* (light) around and I had to climb the staircase. The feelings that came with these dreams assured me that maybe I wouldn't die too soon."

Young, old, sick, grieved, distressed, specially-abled and "deranged", all devotees of Imam Hussein come and beseech God in this sacred space, thwarting questionable perceptions, not so uncommon in the imagination of people who vehemently oppose the concept of shrines in Kashmir and elsewhere. To Jiji, this contention of faith "cannot be handled with mere rationality" as the experiences of sincere devotees are "visceral" about the connection they feel in their hearts, like hers.

"My medication for cancer would not have cured the pain and fear in my heart and the feelings I felt during that time. This shrine did that part of healing for me, when I wouldn't know where to seek help."

Jiji has never missed a single Muharram gathering in the shrine, when she would not be present for prayers. Growing up and old in the shrine's compound, she witnessed miracles in the place that made her connection with her creator stronger. She would come to the shrine every Thursday after her marriage, years before she was diagnosed with cancer.

Jiji's father and my grandfather, Papaji, would recite poetry and salutations for the grandsons of the Prophet during Muharram gatherings inside the shrine. "Once Papaji's acquaintance from some state in India had come to visit the shrine; he went inside and sat in the inner sanctum while we waited for him outside. Hours passed and he was nowhere to be seen. We went inside and saw him frozen in his prayers. No one felt it appropriate to break his prayers. Hours later, he came out to revel in a state of elation and awe that he had seen Imam Hussein in a flash of a vision he had inside."

I flag questions my generation faces based on the pervasion of a different religious thought that doesn't root in the "visceral" Jiji speaks of, as a result of which many accuse this tradition of "deviation" with too much exaggeration of love and devotion.

Jiji answers with her lived wisdom of experience that carries a cultural, social and political history, "People of your generation are too divided to understand, rather feel, how this conviction of love is created; they cast their doubts based on 'rote-rationality'."

She decries the perceptions that do not understand the relevance of such symbols and traditions that speak back to the historical and cultural needs of Kashmir. "You people question as simple a thing as *niyaz*.[21] When I was a teenager, labourers used to commute through the city and couldn't afford food while travelling. But when they visited places, it was a common practice for people to take out food in niyaz frequently outside shrines. Many of these labourers would not go back hungry. We used to feed so many unknown people, including poor and hungry travellers, in the compound of Alam Sahib. Your generation would tell me, it's 'nonsense' to do so," Jiji laughs, perchance at the "rationality" of my generation that has gone too far from the conviction with which she reveres the cultural wisdom of Kashmir of her memories.

"Right around the vicinity of the *astaan* (shrine) where the martyrs' graveyard is also located, people would gather whenever drought or any calamity would hit; people would offer special prayers and the Almighty would grant the collective requests for respite."

A generation apart, I rarely witnessed any such gathering for special prayers that Jiji spoke about. Also missing is the conviction with which she believes that their prayers would translate after a religious ritual. However, we are connected by a memory we share from the 2000s when the valley simmered with political agitations again. Hundreds of protestors gathered around the vast expanse of the Eidgah and passed through the compound of the astaan. I would peek through the window looking over the astaan and processions. Indeed, my association with the place is political, while Jiji's political association with the place is not divorced from the spiritual.

---

21 A religious consecration of food, shared among people.

11

What does it mean to be an ordinary working-class woman from the city?

Nairu Naqsh

1. Wake up at *Fajr* Namaz or sometimes even earlier to knead piles of dough for the large joint family. As soon as the dough is done, roll the rotis and cook them. There is a reason to do it super early. Cooking would mostly be done on subsidised cook stoves called heaters in the local parlance. These heaters have replaced the *chulhas* (mud ovens) and kerosene stoves. As the subsidised electricity ran erratically, cooking whenever electricity was available, often in the wee hours of the night, was necessary. Most of the time, lunch would also be cooked and wrapped in thick layers of old tweed pherans.

Though there are bakers in the city who bake bread for breakfast, how would an *ayaldar* (someone with a big family) afford the baker's bread? The quantity of bread needed for the vast family would surpass the budget, so the women decided to make rotis at home. Besides, there is a lot of *Barkat* in making bread at home. In Kashmir, Barkat entails abundance, deriving more from a lesser monetary value.

2. Clean and mop the house and wash clothes manually daily. So much so that the weathered hands looked like crumpled tissue paper; one would go on washing the patios and other adjoining areas with absolute reverence.

3. Never care about the calluses and corns on your feet because they are not to be cared for. You look at them each month and want to do something about them, but you don't. Because time spent on self-care is something unheard of. *Panas waatun* (self-care) entails buying a home bleach kit or Afghan snow fairness cream once or twice in marriage season. As it lightens the facial hair, it gives an instant fair glow. Remember, being fair is essential.

4. Enjoy sweet tea and biscuits at 10.00 a.m. with lively banter. Everything stops at this moment. If one was conscious about appearances, one would take the time to comb one's hair, but would eventually give in and work. Sometimes, chaff off the rice or grind other condiments for the kitchen, like chillies, turmeric, ginger and fennel. In between, attend to numerous guests who came with their demands, like asking for kehva. No guest was offended and offered whatever they desired. The guests ranged from relatives to beggars to matchmakers.

The arrival of autumn also meant preparing the coal and sawdust for winter kangris. The winter temperatures prevented one from leaving this job for later. Quintals of rice were also stored in seed bins for the upcoming winters.

Seasonal acquaintances also came visiting and had to be attended to, like the kangri seller who came in late autumn or the plum and apricot seller who came in mid-summer. One would have to find time to listen to their stories and what went on with them since they last met because otherwise, they might be offended.

5. As the day progresses and lunchtime arrives, fill copper vessels with mounds of rice and thin curry. It is understood that rich

Artwork by Salman Khursheed

people could enjoy thick curries while the poor would have to do with thin ones. *Gurbat* (poverty) decided its menu. The men, the old, and the guests were given soft, fluffy rice, while the women had leftovers from the night before or crusty rice left at the bottom of the cooking vessel. On occasional days when there was meat on the menu, guests got the choicest cuts, followed by men of the family, and then eventually women. However, such days were rare. Later, industrial poultry production increased the number of days that chicken was served.

6. Enjoy a siesta after lunch and wash dishes, or jump to spinning yarn, knitting, *aari* embroidery, or tile work. This exercise was income-generating, so it had to be taken seriously. Many women finished household chores as early as possible and spent the rest of the day doing this.

7. Go for occasional visits to relatives, walking to and fro most of the time. The city was small, so making these journeys on foot was possible. On reaching the household of relatives, enjoy the salted tea with homemade rotis or a knot of baker's bread or, if lucky, maybe a bakery item. Tea back at home would also be served with homemade rotis or *Soet*, a kind of dry roasted flour made of maize or rice and soaked in salted tea till it swelled. It is usually filling and gives a thick texture to the watery tea. Poverty decides its menu, as I wrote earlier. But if you are a guest, thicker tea with cream would be served.

8. Visit shrines in the city, offering obeisance and tying knots for wishes which could not be spelt out to someone else. There is a strange connection to the shrine where one could cry out and confide in the saint. Then there are shrine friendships, developed and nurtured within shrines, going a long way sometimes. The beauty of these friendships is the organic connection, without any forceful reciprocity or the burden of taking these friendships outside the shrine.

9. Attend occasional weddings, wear good clothes, not fineries, join the camaraderie, help open brides' plaits and sing collectively in laughter and joy. The happiness is nicely curated and goes back to one's world. To join the *wazwan* feast, pack all the meat and chicken items in polythene bags. Four people share a large plate during the feast, but with women, one hardly sees them enjoying

the meats other than the starter spreads like *methi maaz*, chutneys or curries. They enjoy morsels of food with different curries, which fills them nicely. They often chuckle around, loosening their trouser cords because they feel so full.

10. Collect fine items but do not use them. If unmarried, keep them for later when one is married, and if married, keep them for your daughters—collecting hard-earned money from spinning yarn or other handicraft work and fetching fine items from far off. If someone were visiting Ladakh, he would be given money to bring velvet. Similarly, if someone were going to Hajj, the person would be asked to get fabric from there. These fabrics were safely kept in trunks with naphthalene balls till the movement of marriage arrived.

Young girls blushed at the sight of these fineries, imagining how beautiful they would look and how they would garner appreciation from their husbands. Sometimes, the makeup collected would expire before the wedding arrived, but it did not matter.

One wore the fineries only at a wedding to save them for their unborn daughters. The fineries were meant to live in trunks until cloth moths tore them apart. It often fuelled a storm in the family when it had to be decided whom the (*jadaad*) jewellery should be kept with and how it should be used later. Sometimes, it was saved for children but used primarily for familial needs, such as for a sister-in-law's wedding or making a new house. Women always thought they owned jadaad, but did they own it? I wonder.

11. Wear the most uncomfortable footwear because the concept of comfortable footwear never reached you, or perhaps sometimes indulge in ugly Bata flats.

12. Kill your desires every day when you see people around you dressed fancily but choose a printed cheap material for your clothes and wear it irrespective of what is in fashion. Get it stitched by a tailor who charges less but is not versatile with his cuts and creases. Despite knowing that 180 meters away, an array of tailors are known for their crafts, but because they charge more, you don't spend on yourself.

13. Live without personal space all your life and share rooms with siblings/cousins or other women of the household before marriage.

The rooms they share with their husbands after marriage are the first time they get rooms to themselves. But culturally, one is supposed to spend time in the living areas in the day and go to bedrooms only at night. One is supposed to spend waking hours in the presence of everyone from the household. Sometimes, to escape the crackdown of eyes, move to the *kaeni* (roof attics) for spinning yarn, knitting, embroidering, or to enjoy a personal moment.

14. Pray to revered saints and Sufis for health, safety, security and good times to come.

Artwork by Umaid Niyaz

4

Shelters of Solace

12

Shergarhi Complex

Fatima Masnoon

The Shergarhi Complex is located in Jehangir Chowk along the river Jehlum. It came into being during Afghan rule as they decided to move their Governor's residence outside the limits of *Shehr-e-Khaas*. The move is said to have been driven by the desire to reduce the power and importance of Shehr-e-Khaas by moving the seat of power to the periphery and thus guiding a pattern of development and movement of people out of the inner-city core.

Afghan rule is considered a negative period in Kashmir's history, with their rule being despotic and oppressive. The Afghans were a destructive regime that destroyed some of the Mughal gardens, although they built the Amira Kadal and the Shergarhi complex along with the Hari Parbat fortifications. The location of the complex was strategic being along the Jehlum, since water transport was the major means of communication with the rest of the world. The digging of Kut-i-Kul as well as the presence of Tchunth Kul on the opposite bank gives the location protection against floods as well.

The palace was constructed by Amir Khan Jawan Sher, hence the name Shergarhi. The palace built here by the Afghans is long gone and, in its place, stands the Dogra palace. Since Jehlum was a major transport route, the palace located along it could exert a sense of grandeur and supremacy over anyone who travelled along the route.

The complex has developed over the years with buildings being added as well as destroyed with each successive regime.

The present complex mainly consists of heritage buildings from the Dogra rule, including a part of the palace, a mandir, an office building, and a treasury building. Apart from these, the new additions include three permanent buildings and other small temporary structures. During Dogra rule, the complex acted as the Maharaja's residence and administrative centre. The Gadadar temple was built solely for the royal family's use.

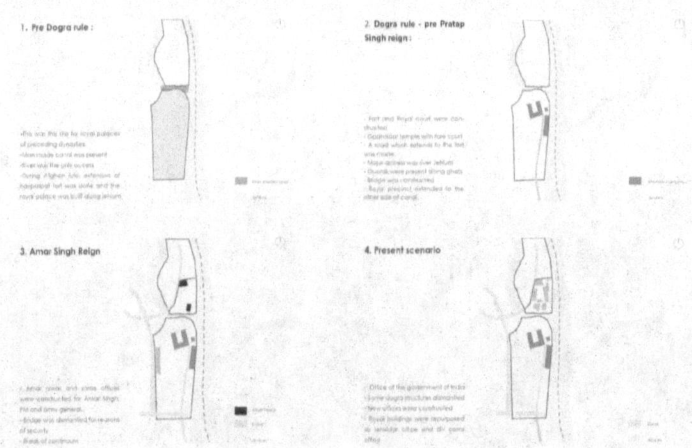

Development of the complex over the years

The complex and its surroundings subsequently developed as administrative centres for Kashmir. During Dogra rule, petitioners used to reach the opposite ghat and ring a bell near the mandir via a rope. One by one these petitioners were called upon and their pleas were heard. Apart from this, the Maharaja used to address gatherings of people from the stone pavilion in the centre of a quadrastyle garden located beyond the palace. After Independence, the complex was used as a secretariat until a new one was developed nearby. It still houses offices of different government departments. The presence of this complex over the years developed the surrounding Lal Chowk area into an administrative hub with the High Court, the Election Commission, the District Commissioner office and the new secretariat offices located around it.

The complex has an air of authority that dominates its heritage aspects. Public access to the complex is limited. The people of Srinagar associate this complex with authority. The multiple security checks and the presence of an army camp within the complex have diminished its heritage aspects. The complex is both physically and visually inaccessible from all sides. Large GI (galvanised iron) sheet walls flank its border along the Jehlum creating a visual barrier. The loss of river transportation has rendered the ghat completely useless and in shambles; it is being used as a dumping site for the waste from the complex.

Roadside view of the complex. Photograph by Author.

*View from the inside. GI Sheets are blocking the view towards Jehlum.
Photograph by Author*

Chinar Bagh within the complex. Photograph by Author.

The complex consists of a large number of chinars along with a proper Chinar Bagh. It is the only open green space situated in the concrete urban development of Jehangir Chowk. However, the presence of visual barriers has left it unknown to most people. The only people aware of it are those who come to the family court operating from a small structure located in the Bagh, thus leaving it entirely unused and unexplored.

Front façade of the palace. Photograph by Author.

Administrative building with the stone pavilion in front of it.
Photograph by Author

Chinar Bagh. Photograph by Author

The palace had an atmosphere of grandeur associated with the seat of supremacy, solidifying the might and power of the Dogras through it. A double flight of steps led up from the ghat to the palace.

The part of the palace that remains standing used to be the durbar or assembly hall, built along the lines of the House of Commons in England, consisting of three large double-storeyed halls with elaborate papier-mache ceilings, reflecting a combination of colonial and local architectural techniques.

Another building that housed administrative offices beautifully reflects the architecture of Kashmiri houses (having the *Taq* system on the ground floor and *Dhajji-deewari* on the upper floor) with a ground floor of stone masonry and upper floors of brick masonry. It is a large building with its planning based along the lines of colonial architecture.

Abandoned Structure. Photograph by Author

A completely abandoned building, which used to house the treasury on the other end of the complex, is a magnificent example of European architecture in Kashmir with different types of gothic windows adorning each floor along with beautifully carved brick masonry.

A little walk from the Shergarhi complex takes us to the Food Corporation of India (FCI) godowns located in Shaheed Gunj. The area was a Rose Garden created by the Mughals for their queens, and was known as Gulab Bagh. The transition to its use as food storage godowns occurred during Dogra rule. This transition reflects how the art and architecture of a place changes with changing rulers. The destruction of buildings created by previous rulers is often seen as a way for the new ruler to assert their dominance and develop political hegemony.

The original godowns were wooden; later, masonry structures were added. It was accessed from the Kut-i-Kul canal that runs along its eastern edge. The ration was transported to ghats via boats along the canal. It was stored in godowns and then distributed among people from here.

Old Timber godowns. Photograph by Author

Heritage building. Photograph by Author.

The heritage building currently housing FCI offices used to act as a horse stable with rooms for caretakers. It is a beautiful brick building with large windows and arched verandahs which have been partially covered in some places to create more space for the office building. The walls are thick corresponding to the taq system of construction native to Kashmir. Its architecture is such that the rooms remain cool even during the hottest months of summer, thus exemplifying the sustainability and contextual credibility of vernacular architecture. The building also has skylights, which are rare in Kashmiri architecture.

Garden within the complex. Photograph by Author.

The amount of open space in the complex is a surprise to the person entering it from the congested streets of Shaheed Gunj. The presence of government offices implies that only the people who visit these offices know about it. The entire complex is secluded and sealed off from the bund through the use of high walls thus leaving it physically and visually inaccessible. All the same, children from local communities playing cricket between the abandoned godowns.

Most parts of the complex are unused and abandoned thus creating negative spaces within the fabric of the city, which can be used for illegal activities.

However, it must be said in conclusion that even though the Shergarhi Complex has been a symbol of power through much of its lifetime, lately, the complex and adjoining structures are finally being used as commons by neighbouring residents. After years of being a site of authority, the complex is at last emerging as a shelter of solace.

13

Loitering Through the Multicultural Neighbourhoods of Lal Chowk

Sabiqa Wani

I did not know that Lal Chowk had multicultural neighbour-hoods or, for that matter, any neighbourhoods till that day; I opened my Instagram and saw that *Her Pixel Story*, a collective of Kashmiri women photographers bringing distinct visual narratives from Kashmir, and *Yaadgah*, a collective working on memory in the old city, were organising a walk around Lal Chowk. It sounded exciting, and I quickly registered, not knowing this walk would change my perspective of the city centre and, most importantly, of walking around it. Honestly, I was unsure if one could ever loiter in this congested city centre.

Photograph taken during walk around Lal Chowk

I come from a traditional Kashmiri family, and we lived roughly 20 kilometres from Lal Chowk. My relationship with Lal Chowk was limited, built through shopping experiences in Goni Khan, an all-ladies bazaar. One would enter the bazaar and be taken over by the colours of fabrics and dupattas hanging from the shop fronts. However, what marked this relationship was a strange sense of calculated time: 10 minutes from the bus yard to the bazaar, 40 minutes in the bazaar and then quickly heading back home. It was unsaid that 'good' women don't loiter and return home promptly after finishing work. Besides, the political volatility of Lal Chowk always loomed large over one's trip to the city centre. But the volatility also applied to men, who would therefore not accompany us.

When I joined a higher secondary school closer to the city centre, the frequency of trips to Lal Chowk increased, sometimes taking quite long and blaming the city traffic or making excuses that one was accompanying a friend for a chore. However, by then, the city was also expanding, and new spots for hanging out had come up. But the question persisted: are women allowed to access these spaces freely, without a sense of fear of having being seen by one of the relatives or by a mean neighbour who would go home and tell folks that I was spotted there, followed by rounds of verbal questioning why was I there in the first place. Was someone else with me? Was the person known to the family? If the person is known, a phone call would be made to compare the narrative. How would anyone have walked through the city under these circumstances? Somehow, I mustered up the courage on this day and decided to join the walk.

Seeing so many women turning up for the walk, and many photography enthusiasts with their cameras was overwhelming. Some of them were history buffs and architecture enthusiasts. However, what held this group together was the fire in their eyes of having won over a matrix of situations that would withhold their right to wander and claim the city. It was a motley group of women who wanted to understand the city as few of its inhabitants would do, memorising the city with their feet. Every corner and alley could plunge us into a trance on this sunny September day. As the narrator of the walk took us through lanes and by-lanes, talking about what happened here and what the place epitomised, we tuned ourselves to the idea of the new freedom of knowing the city not through its literature or its food but by walking. For many of us, an exercise like this would have felt eccentric earlier. Still, here we were, only glimpsing the unofficial history of the city, halving the historical epochs neatly through architecture and what was left behind. From the Sikh era to the Dogra era to British residency times, residues and textures were waiting to be found. Some of us noted everything we saw, wondering who had walked the squares before us. Suddenly, life was not imbued with a sense of the future tense, and we parked ourselves in the present. We drifted between our phone camera lenses and the realities that waited for us, like the sight of a decaying wall or Victorian window boxes which must have been covered with flowers at some point. Sometimes, a thing as quotidian as a grid in the street appeared exemplary. We were collectively satisfied that the day belonged to us and we did not have to be anywhere else.

Another marked feature that came out that day was walkability. Lanes and streets that never felt walkable offered space to us, even though Srinagar is not a city that offered a great deal of walkability. Somewhere, the town's planners relinquished the idea of making a city walkable in favour of motorcars. Or they planned the city for social apathy. You never walked the streets, so it was easier to look away from the plight of many who were perhaps not as privileged as we are.

Then, there were questions about differential access to the city depending on one's position and location. Are cities planned to keep middle-class virtues in view? I began asking myself. What was not considered safe for me has always been safe for fisherwomen who make sales on roads and make a decent living. Or, for that matter, women who beg and live on the streets. In Kashmir, we also have a long history of *maetsce* (women who crossed over the defined mental parameters) who roamed and lived on streets as if they owned them. We have folklore about the Kashmiri mystic Lal Ded wandering from village to village naked or nearly naked, singing songs of enlightenment. More recently, Kashmiri women have been championed as politically vocal and have participated in political processions, marching during the Quit Kashmir movement and joining the women's militia of the National Conference. But I wonder who these women are, and how they navigated between the home and the street. Another example that crosses my mind is The Association of Parents of Disappeared People (APDP); the members would sit in a public park every month, protesting against the disappearance of their loved ones. APDP has been a compelling movement, but I wonder if it would have been as robust and respectful if the cause they stood up for was not socially sanctioned. Would it have been so easy for them to claim the public parks?

Photograph taken during walk around Lal Chowk

I think it is worthwhile to ask what kind of spaces women have access to and what kind of spaces they are barred from, or to redefine the matter of which spaces can be accessed without functional invisibility. For that matter, the fisherwoman, the beggarwoman or the maetsce live through functional invisibility given their location and place. Others are compelled to demonstrate a legitimate reason to be where they are, commuting to work, ferrying children to school bus stops, and doing groceries. Or strategising consciously or unconsciously about navigating public space, like clubbing several chores together to reduce the number of occasions one goes out of the house. Even though many women have joined the workforce and drive their way through the streets, negotiations persist.

The walk somehow opened my mind to the multiple lives and worlds of most Kashmiri women. They navigate the compartmentalised matrix of home and outside on a daily basis, jostling between visibility and invisibility, pretending they are busy either talking on the phone or listening to music. Their body language shows classic postures of defensiveness. Their freedom is subject to knowing their limits, restrictions that often don't apply to men.

Meanwhile, my phone rings, and I have to tell my family where I am and why I am here. I move to a smaller alley to talk and find some other participants on their phones. Our eyes meet, and we share smiles, knowing that we were in the process of finding our own territories.

14

An Ode to Court Road

Arshi Javaid

I have been trying to write about life in Court Road for a while. However, I am yet to be successful. I have written short personality snippets on rough notes, tissue papers, and back covers of diaries that occasionally pop up from my desk corners, bags, and jacket pockets in different cities I shuttle between. I regret not having a concise diary or a pencil for my iPad where I could have written occasionally whenever memory permitted. Though Court Road beats inside me like a second heart, writing about it requires me to go into a specific mood where I have to leave the vagaries of modern life, sip cups of chai, devour soaked kulchas,[22] relax my every nerve, and engage in the process of remembering. Many days, a triggering object reminds me of Court Road; a conversation or a dream, but then, the industrial clock defies everything. A deadline, meal preparation, a meeting, an anxiety attack, and the chain of thought breaks.

I was born in Court Road, Lal Chowk, in the late 1980s, nearly at the same time militancy emerged in Kashmir. As Lal Chowk was the city centre, my family, like others, was in drift and disarray, given the political volatility that they suddenly encountered. The militant movement was urban-centred initially before it moved to other districts. Kashmir Liberation Front (KLF), the first militant organisation, had an urban base and operated in working-class neighbourhoods. Their cadre also mostly belonged to working-class families, and while growing up, it was common to hear someone's first cousin or someone's son was with KLF. In some ways, it was like a neighbourhood welfare organisation, which people associated with in one way or another. However, being close to the geographical centre of the organisation meant a lot of chaos and anarchy, protests and stone pelting, tear gas

22 Kashmiri Kulcha is a shortbread of sorts baked using Ghee that gives it a crumbly crunchy texture.

shells, and batons. There was always a sense of disturbance around us; the precarity of being caught in one of the stone-pelting incidents or something more significant.

Photograph by Arshi Javaid

Various events from this time were transmitted to me so many times that they became a part of my core memory, like when militants blasted the CID central office in our mohalla, escaped through our courtyard, and later, the police dogs sniffed around. Or how ammunition was transported in boats from the bund side. I was six months old at that time. I am unsure if my family had seen it or acquired this information through someone else's narrative. Given my family's love for stories, it would not be hard to imagine that many were collected narratives. In fact, not only was my family inclined to stories, but our entire mohalla had a particular penchant for stories. For example, Nehru promised a plebiscite to Shiekh Mohammad Abdullah in front of the cheering crowds about 100 metres away from our mohalla. Every other person narrated this incident as eyewitnesses when they were born decades later. Or when Shiekh Mohammad Abdullah was arrested in 1953, women from our mohalla, including my Boba (grandmother), were protesting for days and nights. She had some money on her, which she used to buy *chana-chole* and enjoyed her freedom till the money lasted.

Court Road was a haven for story connoisseurs. Retrospectively, stories were part of the inner sanctum that kept the people sane amidst the commotion and noise outside the mohalla, which also had a political tenor. So, whatever happened outside was balanced with the banter inside.

Let me geographically locate Court Road for those who don't know where it is. An amalgam of several small mohallas (Pahri Bal, Kawji Bagh, Hammam Kocha, Gurudwara Gali and the bund), it became Court Road much later when the Dogras built the District Court. If you are walking from Hari Singh High Street through the Amira Kadal, which was the first bridge built by Amir Khan Jawan Sher, you will encounter the bund on the right. Walk a few footsteps on the bund, take any of the four stone staircases to your left, and walk towards a more expansive square towards the gurudwara. The houses in and around are Pahri Bal and the Bund Mohalla. If you instead walk straight from Amira Kadal towards the gurudwara, built during Sikh rule, and take a right, then one would land at the Gurudwara Gali and walk straight to Kawji mohalla (the mohalla of cremators, which has been there since the days of Buddhism in Kashmir). Another more extensive lane connects the square of Lal Chowk to the court premises and functions as Court Road for most people. The Kawji mohalla is built on a raised platform, flat on the top, where corpses would be brought and cremated. Later, the ashes would be immersed in the Jehlum River, a few metres away.

Cremators were among the first to settle in this mohalla. However, their population dwindled with time. Perhaps the changing religious landscape of Kashmir led to the decline of certain occupational groups, or structural changes became a reason for moving occupations. Surprisingly, the last remaining cremator, a Muslim, passed some three decades ago. The population inflow during various ruling dispensations influenced the settlement patterns on Court Road. During the Afghan era, when Amir Khan Jawan Sher constructed Amira Kadal, he sought the help of a local community of Hanjis instead of the nobility. Possibly, some portion of the population who came to help with the bridge settled in and around.

Similarly, Gurudwara Singh Sabha was established during Sikh rule to cater to the soldiers from the barracks around the now Goni Khan market. Over the years, the presence of the Gurudwara made it possible for the Sikh population to find the area relatable and live there, even if temporarily. In 1871, new markets—Goni Khan and Hari Singh High Street—were set up. Punjabi Khatri merchants from Amritsar predominantly ran these markets. While the more moneyed Khatris resided towards Hazoori Bagh, Magarmal, and Gogji Bagh, the working-class population hovered towards Lal Chowk and its neighbourhoods. There were some white-collared Hindu families as well who had chosen to live towards the bund side, which is how Court Road got its Hindu population. Hindu and Sikh Partition refugees joined in 1947, temporarily or permanently, depending on where livelihood opportunities took them later. Likewise, Sikh families escaping Delhi and Lucknow came after the 1984 anti-Sikh riots.

Court Road also had a small Buddhist population who came fleeing after the People's Republic of China invaded Tibet. While the Muslim Tibetan population settled in areas of Hawal and Eidgah, the Buddhist population chose to live near the city centre, where they could find livelihood options as well. Through the sale and knitting of woollens, they restarted their lives. In the 1980s, some Muslims arrived from Assam and adjoining areas who had escaped the Nellie massacre. Seasonal visitors, such as the Banjara community, came and lived in makeshift tents through the summer and left by early autumn. Their arrival exposed me to the caste and class question in Hinduism quite early on, which led to a realisation that the same questions existed within Islam too, albeit in different forms. While Muslims spoke to Banjaras, the Punjabi Hindus hesitated.

When I write about a multi-religious and multi-cultural presence in Court Road, it does not necessarily mean that there was a dense population of a particular community. However, it was a presence that prepared one for knowledge about the other, and possibly, acceptance. This acceptance was not propagated outright, but through co-living in subtle ways. This is not to say that minorities would not have their challenges, which I, as a privileged member of the majority community, would not perceive or acknowledge.

Going back to co-living, Court Road absorbed everyone who came to it and became a part of its story. After a while, it hardly mattered who came from where. People became intertwined in each other's lives, and new narratives came to the fore. I am equally mindful of not presenting a rosy picture to satiate my creative impulses. Perhaps the working-class force nurtured a sense of "live and let live", or maybe there was so much happening outside that you needed a breather once you walked into the neighbourhood. I always found a compelling sense of acceptance in my family and neighbourhood.

We had inherited our house from our grandfather, who had also reached here after several migrations from different parts of Kashmir. The last spot was South Kashmir. Grandfather and his elder brother had made a fortune in the timber business and decided to move to an urban location to expand their network. They moved to Srinagar and bought land on Court Road, where they constructed two huge houses with 32 rooms, four huge balconies, six cellars, and multiple attics. They also made a smaller house for their sister in the same courtyard. However, as the winds changed and fortunes fell, the same property was used for renting purposes. For the most part, our renters had been Partition-affected Punjabi families, a Sikh family and a Hindu family from Banaras. The Punjabi families left during militancy and migrated to Jammu and Delhi, but the Sikh family and the Hindu family stayed behind over my childhood and adulthood. Given the Partition and migration background, the Punjabi families were Jana Sangh supporters who also went to *shakha* on Sundays, but it did not seem to bother the Muslim landlords. It was often said they could have their reasons to align with the party. It never translated into hostility of any kind, as both parties knew they stood on opposing planks on this front. Our mohalla also had a few government alcohol shops. In Muslim-majority contexts like Kashmir, drinking is not socially permissible, but many in our mohalla, Muslims and non-Muslims alike, enjoyed their drink after sunset. In the storytelling tradition of the mohalla, it was not an issue of contention as long as people remained sober. It was often said, "*Sharaab chu chewaan, magar panie gharie, panen pounsan*" (The person drinks but in his own house, with his own money). As children, this would appear as another punchline, but now, this approach seems generous when I see the hate politics around food and drink.

A certain genuineness existed around inter-personal relations as well. For example, our Maulvi Sahib, who had come in after the Nellie massacre and joined the local mosque, had become friends with the religious minorities. It was not a relationship developed for proselytisation, but a genuine respect for another human life and their faith, so much so that the minorities from the mohalla often visited him for spiritual healing. Maulvi Sahib smiled and helped without raising questions about their faith. Rama, daughter of Chunni Lal, who had died by suicide due to debt, found a strange solace in Maulvi Sahib's presence. She had suffered because of her parent's suicide and the loneliness that followed. With the inability to find a partner, Rama ran a tea stall by day and wandered on empty roads at night. Winters could still calm her, but summers were a time of rage for her. The suicide of her parent would become the dominant memory in summer, and Rama would scream at the top of her voice and chase people with kitchen knives. Nobody could handle her through this save for Maulvi Sahib, whose kind look would make her drop the knives and return to routine work and sanity.

Another person hugely influenced by Maulvi Sahib was Master, who came from Odisha as a child. Nobody knew why and how he reached here. He found a job with a tailor where he learnt the craft. Master was a practising Hindu all his life, but visited Maulvi Sahib for guidance. Maulvi Sahib's daughter Reshma had a best friend, Naina, who was Sikh, and spent most of the time in the masjid compound lazing, playing, and planning activities. Reshma also went to Naina's house to watch television and dance to Bollywood songs. Both went to different schools: Naina to an Arya Samaji school and Reshma to a school run by an Islamic endowment. However, affection between the two superseded everything else. After two decades, Maulvi Sahib returned to his native place as his parents needed him. Master died of cancer in 2019, but requested that he be buried in the mohalla graveyard as people would visit him. Some say Master had conformed to Islam a year before his death. Rama died in 2023 after being in and out of the mental asylum for years.

Strange encounters marked daily life in Court Road. My octogenarian grandmother, who could not speak a word beyond Kashmiri, somehow found ways to communicate with this Sikh lady who had been renting a place in our compound for the last six decades. The Sikh lady lived by herself after the death of her husband and the marriage of her daughter. She only spoke Punjabi. She ran a tattered cosmetics shop in one of the former Pandit neighbourhoods, but could hardly make ends meet. The makeup she sold was often outdated and expired, and her buyers had migrated. No money came in, but the shop and house rent had to be paid. Though she never talked about it to anyone, the gold rings on her fingers kept disappearing. She had always lived a modest life, but now things worsened. Her daily menu was reduced to *namak walay chawal, namak wali roti,* and *chai* (salted rice, salted bread, and tea). Some elders in the family noticed it and decided she should not be asked to pay the rent, and her rent should not be increased. A lifetime rental cap was imposed on her case. Whenever she had money, she could pay. She continued paying 200 rupees for a two-bedroom apartment and balcony in a prime location until she stayed in Kashmir, probably around 2016, after which she went to live with her daughter in Amritsar. Old age was becoming unmanageable, and some of her close gurudwara friends who kept her company had died as well. Her final farewell was very painful for her and us, sealing a lifetime spent together. Despite this, we are regularly in touch by phone.

Before phones arrived in Court Road, home-grown networks kept us connected. My differently abled cousin Bashir founded his supreme network, which operated without wires or devices. He ensured that all the gossip and political news reached everyone around us. Bashir had his internal calendar of where to go on which day and which relative to visit to gather information. He mostly walked through the city, sometimes asking for a lift from bikers or auto drivers as he never had any money. He was quick and crisp with his craft, never wasting time, and his eyes and ears were always on high alert. However, like all detectives and spies, he had a weakness: his love for tea, which derailed him from many of his self-assigned tasks. In those moments, his opponents would triumph over him. They were mainly beggars who roamed around the city and knew what was happening where. In one instance, when the Gyaani of the Gurudwara was arrested after being identified as a Pakistani spy, Bashir lost to a beggar due to indulgence in tea. He had stopped at his maternal home for one extra cup of tea. The defeat haunted him for a long time, and he hated beggars after this.

Landline phones reached Muslim households in Court Road much later than our Hindu Punjabi neighbours because they were traders and had business connections and families outside the valley. They allowed us to come and attend calls, and if urgent, to make some as well. The calls we went to receive were short, often affirmative, and the calls that we made were even shorter because everyone said that making phone calls was expensive. Nobody knew how expensive they were, but everyone said that. I had the chance to attend a phone call once with my paternal cousin sister, whose family had called. The conversation was brief, without pauses, squeezed to eight words, *"Mithaw gharie ter zi ni, military che sersie"* (Mitha don't come home, the military is everywhere).

On our way back, amidst the tension, we noticed a small, frail woman sitting silently on her verandah, knitting her sweater. Unlike other Hindu neighbours, she was not very pleasant to Muslims or even her co-religionists. As she lived alone in a vast mansion, children called her *bhoot* (ghost). My cousin told me her siblings had moved abroad. Originally from Kishtawar Valley, Tara's ancestors were appointed to look after the law-and-order function during the Mughal era. They had lived in Srinagar ever since, and at some point, her parents moved into Court Road. They named their eldest daughter Tara, who shone like her name. With a university degree, she quickly found a secure job. Given her personal and familial profile, finding a match for her would not have been difficult. But Tara had fallen for a man who could not have married her. A prodigal son of a rich man, he visited her when he needed to find himself, away from the madness and noise of the outer world. Gradually, he was directed to politics and business, which perhaps wasn't his calling. To find respite, he visited Tara, who cooked elaborate meals, and they enjoyed listening to the radio together. Over the years, he kept visiting, and Tara kept loving without a promise of permanence. Elders in the neighbourhood say that he kept visiting till his political and familial life took over, and it was unsafe for him to have an alternate life. Gradually, as his visits thinned and then stopped, Tara began withering. She lost weight, her hair greyed, and her eye sockets completely sank. She also dressed only in white and never played the radio again. Tara died in 2022.

As the political uncertainty continued, many Punjabi Hindu families started moving their businesses to Jammu and Delhi. Their fear had not settled after the Partition loss, and they considered moving the women and children outside for a while. Many waited for years till they moved out ultimately. Some of our renters had just left with a handful of belongings, imagining that the return would be soon. However, the return never happened. The Pandit migration and selective killings of Hindus had added to the fear. I remember peeping through the window panes of their deserted houses while their possessions awaited them. Some of them came to collect these as late as the 2000s. In some families, the young left, but the old stayed back. However, many of them were forced to migrate later due to geriatric issues or being left alone after the death of their spouses.

Around the same time, several Muslims also began migrating out of the neighbourhood. The expansion of families and the urge to live in more extensive, gentrified spaces away from commercialisation surfaced. As militancy was rife in urban areas, many people thought moving towards the peripheries and keeping the children away would be wise—so those who could afford left quickly while others dreamt of leaving soon. My own extended family started leaving year after year.

Many boys from working-class families in mohalla had crossed over to Pakistan; their dream of freedom was a dream of a good life that could happen someday. While they wrestled their way through snowy mountains into Pakistan, back in Court Road, we woke up to armed crackdowns and combing operations every day. The boys who pelted stones were sent to faraway detention centres. Though there were extended curfews and strikes throughout the valley, on rare days when there weren't, Lal Chowk would not open. Services, mostly water supply, would be stopped for days. The city centre was being punished for its political stance. However, many could not bear the weight of the economic misery that came along. They defected politically and joined the mainstream chorus, creating political proxies in the area.

The Jehlum beautification project displaced a particular population that lived by the river. The area was criminalised, and the drug peddlers were given a free hand. The downfall of Lal Chowk and the adjoining neighbourhoods seemed like a political project which had to be undertaken to teach a symbolic lesson and mark a particular territory politically.

New dynamics surfaced after the 2014 floods, severely damaging the area's properties. Multiple stakeholders jointly owned most properties that were also non-insured. Hence, any settlement for repair or refurbishing around them was complex. So, in most cases, builders stepped in and acquired the properties from all parties. This rapidly changed the character of the city centre and its neighbourhood.

Lal Chowk's status was further diminished after the abrogation of Article 370 in 2019. It became an embodiment of the Bharatiya Janta Party's Naya Kashmir. Economically emaciated, socially distressed and politically plagued, the imposed urban renewal looks like a dreamwork of authoritarian urbanism. The new clock tower, the Balidhan Stambh,[23] and other symbols of Naya Kashmir pose a confrontation between remembering and forgetting the city, a sanctioned and a non-sanctioned narrative of the city.

My family moved out of Court Road in 2017. I am told that not more than 10 to 15 families continue living there; the rest has been acquired by builders or rented by hawkers, who form a vote bank for a particular mainstream politician. As overbearing as it is to visit Court Road now, it comforts one with its signs of multicultural presence and co-living. A cobblestone might take one into a long reverie of how the Hammam Kocha housed a public bath for soldiers during the Afghan era. A ragged Dhaka Muslin curtain hanging in one of the custodian buildings could tell one about the Muslim Punjabi family it housed before the Partition. Master's shop front still has a board with Hindu symbols, and Tara's huge radio is lying on one of the verandahs of the falling mansion.

---

23 A war memorial constructed in a famous public park in Lal Chowk for honouring the military and paramilitary personnel who have laid down their lives protecting the borders of India.

Bibliography

Foreword by Prof Dr Nadja Christina Schneider

TED Conferences. "Don't ask where I'm from, ask where I'm a local." Featuring T. Selasi. Aired October, 2014.

Introduction

Harvey, David. *Rebel Cities: From the Right to the City to the Urban Revolution*. Verso, 2012.

Said, Edward. *Culture and Imperialism*. Vintage Books, 1994.

Sontag, Susan. *On Photography*. Dell Publishing Company, 1977.

Seeking Home

Home Through My Grandmother's Memory

Assmann, Aleida. "Transformations between History and Memory." Social Research: An International Quarterly 75, no. 1 (March 2008): 49–72. https://doi.org/10.1353/sor.2008.0038.

Celebration of the Present, Mourning the Past, Yearning for the Future

Behar, Ruth. *The Vulnerable Observer: Anthropology That Breaks Your Heart*. Boston, MA: Beacon Press, 1996.

Canning, Charlotte, and Thomas Postlewait. *Representing the Past: Essays in Performance Historiography*. Iowa City: University of Iowa Press, 2010.

Davis, Tracy C. "Performative Time." Representing the Past, 2010, 142–67. https://doi.org/10.2307/j.ctt20mvg5m.9.

Halbwachs, Maurice. *The Collective Memory*. Presses Universitaires de France, 1950.

Kaul, Shonaleeka. *Myths and Places: New Perspectives in Indian Cultural Geography*. Taylor & Francis 2023.

Naikoo, Javaid. "KPs Demand Handover of 13 Temples from Dharmarth Trust." *Early Times*, February 5, 2015. https://www.earlytimes.in/newsdet.aspx?q=148581#.

Press Trust of India (PTI). "Passage of Temple Bill precondition to KPs return to Valley." *India Today*, May 26, 2016.. https://www.india today.in/pti-feed/story/passage-of-temple-bill-pre-condition to-kps-return-to-valley-613585-2016-05-23.

Rai, Mridu. *Hindu Kings, Muslim Subjects: Islam, Rights, and the History of Kashmir.* Princeton University Press, February 2004.

Roach, Joseph R. *Cities of the Dead: Circum-Atlantic Performance.* New York: Columbia University Press, 1996.

Wani, Muhammad A. Islam in Kashmir: Fourteenth to Sixteenth Century. Oriental Publishing, 2004.

Zutshi, Chitralekha. Kashmir's Contested Pasts: Narratives, Geographies, and the Historical Imagination. Oxford University Press, 2014.

Yaarbal

Gender, Leisure and Public Sacred Spaces of Srinagar City

Mazumdar, Shampa, and Sanjoy Mazumdar. 2001. "Rethinking public and private space: Religion and women in Muslim society." Journal of Architectural and Planning Research 18, no. 4 (December 2001): 302–324.

Shelters of Solace

Shergarhi Complex

Alkazi, Feisal. *Srinagar: An Architectural Legacy.* New Delhi: Lotus Collection, 2014.

Razdan, Vinayak. "Sher Garhi Palace as It Was." SearchKashmir, September 4, 2015. https://searchkashmir.org/2015/09/sher garhi-palace-as-it-was.html.

Contributors

Dr Arshi Javaid is an Einstein Junior Scholar at Humboldt-Universität zu Berlin. Before this, she was a critical residency fellow with *AiE* at Freie Universität Berlin, where she curated a collection of first-person narratives exploring the shared everyday life between Kashmiri Muslims and Kashmiri Pandits before 1989. She earned her PhD from Jawaharlal Nehru University, where she focused on the contestation of the Self and the Other in Kashmiri nationalism. Her research has since been developed into a book, *Kashmiri Nationalism, 1989–2016: Contested Politics of 'Self' and 'Other'* published by Transcript Verlag in November 2024. In addition to her work on nationalism, Arshi is deeply engaged with urban spaces' socio-political and cultural dynamics. Her research explores how spatial politics shape political identities, particularly in conflict zones like Kashmir. She investigates how urban spaces in Kashmir act as sites of contestation, memory, and identity, highlighting the complex relationships between space, politics, and identity in these regions.

Adil Malik is pursuing a Bachelor of Visual Arts (BVA) at Kashmir University. His art explores the intersection of humanity and the natural world, using distorted human figures adorned with animalistic elements to provoke contemplation on the complex relationship between humans and the environment. In his paintings, he composes elements from his daily life, experiences, and memories. He usually distorts human figures and composes them with animal bodies as he sees some animal characteristics in humans.

Ayushi Koul is a doctoral candidate in Theatre and Performance Studies at the School of Arts and Aesthetics, Jawaharlal Nehru University, New Delhi. In her work titled *Theatre of Remembrance and Kashmir: Making Events, Performing Identity*, she observes the remains of historic events in the everyday life of Kashmir. In her prior work titled *Mapping Displacement of Performance Genre: Bhand Pather and its Multiple Facets*, she studies the displacement of the cultural landscape of Kashmir through local performance Bhand Pather.

Fatima Masnoon is a passionate architect interested in using architecture as a tool for social good. She appreciates history and design and explores the interplay between architecture, power, and people in her research. Through her work, she aims to highlight the profound political and social impact of architecture on people and hopes to harness its potential for the greater good.

Khateeba Syed is a Kashmiri researcher exploring the intersection of gender, conflict, and performance. Currently working as a Development Practitioner, she focuses on creating safe spaces for women in Kashmir. She holds a Master's degree in Gender Studies, and her research critically examines how religious performances centred around collective grief shape memory, identity, and communal narratives in Kashmir. She also expresses her insights through photography, capturing the intricate realities of her subjects. Her photographic work has been featured in *Maaje Zev*, a feminist literary collective supported by the Maypole Fund grant. Through her writing and visual storytelling, Khateeba aims to elevate the voices of those navigating the complexities of memory and identity in a rapidly changing landscape.

Meher Qadri, a journalist and visual artist and alumni of the VII Academy from Srinagar, constructs a poignant exploration of grief and loss through her work. Her imagery confronts the intersections of memory, erasure, and the human body as a site of conflict. By focusing on post-traumatic experiences and the struggle for survival, her art becomes a critical reflection on how war inscribes itself onto both individual lives and the collective psyche. Influenced by the likes of Baldwin, Sontag, and Didion, Qadri explores memory and grief through a delicate dance between past and present, a choreography of sorrow and resilience. Her photography captures the understated elegance of life, overshadowed by the perpetual storm of conflict. Through her work, Qadri preserves moments that the relentless tide of mainstream media often neglects. Her work is an archive of the overlooked, a testament to the quiet, enduring spirit of those who live in the peripheries of the world's gaze.

Muntaha Amin is a researcher and an independent woman film practitioner. She identifies as a Kashmiri Muslim Woman and tells stories from living this triply marginalised identity. Her debut film, *Siege in the Air*, documents the lived experiences of young Kashmiri women in perpetual precarity and unending lockdowns in Kashmir centring the communication blockade of 2019 post the abrogation of Article 370. She works as a narrative editor, cultural consultant and film practitioner on freelance film and multimedia projects. *Siege in the Air*, premiered at various international film festivals including the Indian Film Festival of Melbourne, IDSSFK Kerala, Kolkata People's Film Festival, 2023 Newcastle University's Memory Studies Conference, etc. The film received the Best Documentary Award at the Himachal Short Film Festival (2022) and was longlisted for the Toto Awards 2023. Muntaha worked as a cultural consultant on the script of an upcoming Australian feature film *Stripey* with the Academy award-winning writer and director of the animated feature Happy Feet, Warren Coleman and his co-writer Steve Abbott.

Nairu Naqsh is a management graduate from Kashmir University with a keen eye for observing the complexities of society. An avid reader and writer, she channels her reflections into thought-provoking narratives that resonate with authenticity. When not immersed in books or penning her thoughts, Nairu tends to her family orchards, balancing her passion for the written word with the practical demands of sustaining her ancestral roots. Her unique perspective bridges the realms of nature and culture, offering a fresh voice grounded in Kashmiri life and tradition.

Prof Dr Nadja Christina Schneider is a Professor of Gender and Media Studies for the South Asian Region at Humboldt-Universität zu Berlin. Her academic journey spans South Asian and Islamic Studies, as well as Modern and Contemporary History, with a specialisation in Area Media Studies. Her work delves into cultural and urban studies, mobility and gender, secularism and religion, and the evolving landscape of new media. In 2016, Schneider served as a visiting professor at Heidelberg University's Chair of Visual and Media Anthropology and was a Feodor Lynen Fellow at the University of Delhi in 2015. She is the co-speaker and project leader of the interdisciplinary initiative *Beyond Social Cohesion - Global Repertoires of Living Together (RePLITO)*, 2021–2024, which examines innovative approaches to social cohesion, funded by the Berlin University Alliance.

Her recent book, *Reimagining Housing, Rethinking the Role of Architects in India* (Heidelberg Asian Studies Publishing, 2024), contributes to the Media and Cultural Studies series and explores housing and architecture in contemporary India.

Sabiqa Wani is a civil engineer by training, who has been diligently preparing for the Civil Services examinations over the past few years. Deeply fascinated by Srinagar—a city close to her heart through her mother's roots—Sabiqa's connection to the place runs deeper than mere geography. Her childhood was marked by imaginative games with her cousins, where they would playfully recreate the social life of Srinagar. This blend of technical expertise and cultural curiosity shapes Sabiqa's unique perspective, reflecting a harmonious balance of ambition, heritage, and nostalgia.

Sadaf Masoodi is a PhD researcher at the University of Kashmir. Previously associated with ActionAid India as a development practitioner, she writes narrative pieces on culture. She works at the intersection of storytelling, academics and social justice.

Salman Khursheed Lone is a Bachelor of Fine Arts (BFA) student at the University of Kashmir. His work reflects deep engagement with cultural identity, societal issues, and personal experiences, often exploring themes of confinement and resilience through unique mediums. Salman is a passionate artist and avid reader who seeks to contribute meaningfully to the contemporary art landscape.

Shajar Lateef is a final year student at the Institute of Music and Fine Arts, University of Kashmir, pursuing his bachelor's degree in visual arts (painting). His art practice traverses various mediums, including painting, printmaking, sculpture, and installation. His work is informed by the forms and themes found in nature and cities of Kashmir, which developed mainly by observing the native flora, fauna and vernacular architecture.

Umaid Niyaz is an applied arts student at Kashmir University and a versatile artist based in Srinagar. His creative expertise spans various digital mediums, including graphic design and digital painting, alongside his proficiency in freehand drawing and charcoal sketching. Umaid's work often reflects a deep connection to Kashmir's cultural and natural landscapes, blending traditional and contemporary styles. He has showcased his talent in local exhibitions and collaborated on several art projects, earning recognition for his innovative approach and meticulous craftsmanship. Passionate about exploring new techniques, Umaid continually experiments with different artistic forms to push the boundaries of his creativity.